# WOMEN IN THE TIME OF AIDS

## Women, Health and the Challenge of HIV

*Gillian Paterson*

ORBIS BOOKS

Maryknoll, New York 10545

The Catholic Foreign Mission Society of America (Maryknoll) recruits and trains people for overseas missionary service. Through Orbis Books, Maryknoll aims to foster the international dialogue that is essential to mission. The books published, however, reflect the opinions of their authors and are not meant to represent the official position of the society.

---

Originally published as *Love in a Time of AIDS* by WCC Publications, World Council of Churches, 150 route de Ferney, 1211 Geneva 2, Switzerland. ISBN: 2-8254-1191-4.

Copyright © 1996 WCC Publications, Geneva, Switzerland

Published in North American by Orbis Books, Maryknoll, NY 10545-0308
Manufactured in the United States of America

---

ORBIS / ISBN 1-57075-106-4

*for Roger*

# CONTENTS

# ACKNOWLEDGMENTS

More than most, this book has been a collaborative effort. The name which appears on the front cover is mine; my task has been to record, as faithfully as I am able, the thoughts, research and experiences of a group which met, in early September 1995, to reflect on the findings of research supported by CMC—Churches' Action for Health, of the World Council of Churches, on the subject of women and health and the challenge of HIV/AIDS. They are all people with practical experience of working with church-related HIV/AIDS programs. Some members were themselves living with the virus.

The group should have been part of the World Council of Churches' (WCC) presence at the NGO Forum at the UN Fourth World Conference on Women in Beijing. But then came tales of confusion in the organization of the Forum, on top of concern that participants living with HIV might encounter problems on entering China, and also in access to medical care if this became necessary. At the last moment, therefore, the venue was shifted to the Christian Medical College, Vellore, in South India.

For friendship and inspiration, and for trusting me to get it right, I thank the following. When you encounter them elsewhere in the pages of this book, their names will appear initially in bold type, **like this.**

Sara Bhattacharji, Professor of Community Health, and Jacob John, Professor of Microbiology, who were our hosts at the Christian Medical College, Vellore, India.

Monica Arancibia, EPES (Educación Popular en Salud) in Santiago, Chile.

Alice Augustine, from the Christian Medical College, Vellore, India.

Cristina Cavalcanti, social anthropologist and writer, from the Brazilian agency ISER.

Terrie and Bob Cowley, from Cambodia, working with Quaker Peace & Service.

Mary Engwau, Uganda Protestant Medical Bureau, Kampala, Uganda.

Nidia Fonseca, from the Secretariat for Services to Family, Women and Children at CLAI, the Latin American Council of Churches, based in Costa Rica.

Cristina Gutierrez, the Chilean AIDS pastor, whose work I visited in the slum areas of Buenos Aires, Argentina.

Mary Jacob, from the Christian Medical College, Vellore, India.

Caroline Kruckow, from the German development agency EZE, which provided the funding for the change of venue.

Maureen Lewis, from Antigua, representing the Caribbean Council of Churches.

Grace Matilda, from the School of Nursing in Calcutta, India.

Grace Nakazibwe, Uganda Protestant Medical Bureau, Kampala, Uganda.

Florence Nali, from All Saints Health Centre near Jinja, Uganda.

Antonia Poma, from Bolivia.

Jenny Roske, from the WCC's CMC—Churches' Action for Health.

Sr. Saramma, from the Christian Medical College, Vellore, India.

Erlinda Senturias, from the Philippines, coordinator of the WCC AIDS program, working in the CMC—Churches' Action for Health.

Anne Skjelmerud, development and gender consultant, from Norway.

Margareta Sköld, from Sweden, executive secretary for Health and Healing in the CMC—Churches' Action for Health.

Jim Thomas, from the Church of Christ in Thailand program in Chiang Mai.

Christopher Tusubira from All Saints Health Centre near Jinja, Uganda.

Rebecca Wasswa, St. John's Mission, Kampala, Uganda.

Helen and Jim Worth, from Portville, New York.

Jaruwan Wutti from the Church of Christ in Thailand program in Chiang Mai.

We must all be grateful to Ana Langerak, director of the WCC's Unit II—Churches in Mission: Health, Education, Witness, who has supported the "Women and Health and the Challenge of HIV/AIDS" process from the beginning, and to Jacob John and Sara Bhattacharji, at the Christian Medical College, Vellore, for taking us in at the last minute, and for the warmth of their welcome.

My own warmest thanks go, in friendship, to Erlinda Senturias, whose idea it was to document the program in this way, and who invited me to do it. I am grateful to Keith Clements and Malcolm Johnson for keeping me going on occasions when I was flagging, and with them, to Lavinia Byrne, Chung Hyun Kyung, Ruth McCurry, Fiona Thomas and John Webber. All seven of them made thoughtful and detailed comments on parts of the text.

I would like to thank my colleagues in the Churches' Commission on Mission and the Council of Churches for Britain and Ireland for their tolerance of my year-long preoccupation with this book. I owe more than they will ever realize to Walter Wink and Billie Alban for our day-long conversation about powers and systems, in June 1995 and to Kevin Kelly for bread-for-the-journey generally. I am grateful to Margareta Sköld and the staff of CMC—Churches' Action for Health for their friendship; to Aruna Gnanadasan, Ana Langerak and Diana Smith from the WCC for their wise comments on the final document; to R.S. Thomas for permission to quote a verse from his poem "Song at the Year's Turning"; and to all the men and women who welcomed me with such warmth and hospitality on my visits to Uganda, Brazil, Argentina and India.

My husband, Roger Feldman, has endured the year without a murmur. I could not have done without his on-the-spot 24-hour-a-day ministry to my computer, or his courage in raising the awkward and (at the time) unwelcome questions I needed to hear. And finally, I am grateful to the congregation of St. Mary of Eton in the East End of London for their support, friendship and prayers during this and other years; and also for teaching me so much about life, and love, and about the things that become possible when you keep on believing in both.

# INTRODUCTION

The Fourth World Conference on Women, taking place in August-September 1995 in Beijing, China, occurred at a moment of radical change in the profile of HIV, the virus that causes AIDS. HIV has been regarded as an infection primarily of men. Now, more and more women are becoming infected. The proportion of women among those newly infected is rising everywhere in the world. According to conservative estimates by the World Health Organization (WHO), over 14 million women will have been infected by the year 2000, against a total global estimate of 30-40 million men, women and children. From being at the periphery of the epidemic, women today are at the center of concern.

Young women are worst affected. The peak age of infection is between 15 and 24, with a female-to-male ratio of two to one in that age group. And as infections rise in women, so do infections in the infants born to them, with about a third of babies born to HIV-infected mothers becoming infected themselves. The route of transmission to women is overwhelmingly through hetero-sexual intercourse. In industrialized countries, where homo-sexual contact and needle sharing used to account for nearly all infections, there is a clear rise in heterosexual transmission. How has this happened?

"The bleak reality," says WHO, "is that the sexual and economic subordination of women fuels the HIV pandemic." This view is supported by grassroots research and endorsed, now, by all responsible international agencies. Its implications are far-reaching. If a woman has no effective control over her own body, then it's no good expecting her to make responsible decisions about her sexuality. If she is poor, then long-term health risks may seem irrelevant in relation to her own or her family's survival. And this in turn explains why prevention strate-gies that are limited to "knowing the facts" and "becoming aware

of the risk" have not succeeded. Where opportunities for transmission are embodied in the social and cultural organization of
communities, then bringing about behavior change will require
more than knowledge of the facts.

At the international level, there has been recognition of the
need for global institutions to come closer to grassroots realities
and the real concerns of people with AIDS. A mini-revolution
has occurred, resulting in the establishment of the UNAIDS
program, sponsored by WHO, UNESCO, UNICEF, UNDP and the
World Bank. UNAIDS is designed to co-ordinate international and
regional efforts, and to relate more closely to the NGO sector.

This, then, is a time of opportunity, a time of change. For
decades now, there has been a growing acceptance in health
and development circles that family and community health is
linked to women's education, and to their ability to control
reproduction and make choices about family spending. Arguments about human rights have also spotlighted the subordinate
position of women in most cultures. But AIDS is different. It
points the finger at the subordinate role of women and suggests
that failure to do something about it will threaten the survival of
the whole community.

Bad news, or good news? For Hippocrates, father of modern
western medicine, a "crisis" or "critical day" was the day when a
physician could decide whether a patient's condition was taking
a good or a bad turn. A crisis in its true sense is a time of opportunity and of decision-making; a time of turning tides; a time
when anything is possible. It's in times of crisis that systems and
cultures are most open to change. In the case of HIV/AIDS, this
may be a *kairos,* or moment of truth. Challenged by the virus,
cultures and systems may, for a brief moment, be open to the
perception that the continued subordination of women is threatening their very life-blood.

This picture is confirmed by the research described in this
book. In Uganda, "Participatory Action Research" (in which the
research population itself decides the objectives, reflects on its
own practices, defines the problems, suggests and implements
solutions, and monitors the results) has spotlighted the subordinate position of women as an entry point for HIV in urban and
rural areas, and has mapped roads to change. In Brazil, cultural
and media attitudes to women are shown to promote stereotypes

which encourage denial of reality. In the shanty towns of Buenos
Aires, women look at how HIV is transmitted and conclude that,
in their context, it is poverty itself that is the sickness.

For the individuals and groups responsible for this research, it
has become clear that HIV/AIDS is a crisis, calling on cultures
and communities to change. But further than that, the virus
points the finger at those international political and economic
factors which hold nations in a stranglehold and, both in the
industrialized and the developing world, have increased the feminization of poverty and made poor communities poorer.

But the final challenge, as the participants in a seminar at
Vellore in South India, where this work was presented, unanimously agreed, is to our churches. The seminar produced the
"Ecumenical Platform of Action" that is reproduced on pages xiv-
xvi. In their own cultures and structures, our churches mirror
the patriarchal social and political biases that contribute to the
subordination of women. The Bible has traditionally been read in
such a way as to affirm these biases. The sexual dimension of
human experience is often denied. Religious morality may be
handed on as a set of rules which has little to do with people's
everyday experience, blocking the way to the development of
mature and living ethical thinking which is relevant to our trou-
bled and confusing times.

In Vellore we tried, in the light of our own work and experience, to wrestle with some of these issues. "All of us," says the
Platform of Action, "found that this work continually challenged
our thinking, our attitudes and our theology, and transformed our
vision." We are not, any of us, the people we were when we set
out. We know more about the world, about ourselves, and about
God. This book aims to say something about the people involved
in the Women and AIDS program itself, to share the insights they
offer, and to put some flesh on the challenges that, in Vellore,
were addressed specifically to our churches.

The book opens by identifying some of the global issues in
women's health. Chapters 2, 4, 5 and 6 are set in Africa, Latin
America and Asia, and describe particular programs and people,
some of which I was privileged to visit myself. Chapter 3—which
follows the Uganda experience, to which it seems particularly
relevant—briefly introduces the concept of "gender analysis."

Chapters 7 and 8 attempt to give structure to the spiritual, ethical and theological issues over which we argued and laughed and wept and dozed and prayed during those hot, happy, exhausting and invigorating South Indian days. To do justice to these conversations would be impossible; a blow-by-blow account of each discussion would reduce to tedium something that was both relevant and fascinating. I hope that those who were part of them will feel I have reflected the core and spirit of our debates, because the perspectives and thoughts offered in these two final chapters are an attempt to share with readers the real crux of the thinking of that unforgettable week, and also the rationale for the Ecumenical Platform of Action it produced.

# ECUMENICAL PLATFORM OF ACTION

## WOMEN'S HEALTH AND THE CHALLENGE OF HIV/AIDS

### Introduction

The HIV/AIDS epidemic is affecting all aspects of people's lives. Economic, social and cultural factors which perpetuate the subordination of women are contributing to the spread of the virus and exacerbating its effects on the lives of women. We acknowledge the excellent work that is being done in many situations, but in general, strategies of prevention and care by governments, churches and non-governmental organizations have so far failed to influence the broader determinants of the situation of women.

What has this to do with the churches?

Where the church is silent in the face of injustice in the lives of the people, it is not being faithful to God's mission. The time has come, then, for the church to examine and assess the extent of its complicity in upholding the social structures that perpetuate women's subordination.

In some parts of the world, for instance, the churches have collaborated in the myth that the transmission of the

AIDS virus is confined to commercial sex workers, homosexuals and drug users. This is untrue, damaging, and needs to be refuted.

This workshop, therefore, was initiated by the World Council of Churches, and held at the Christian Medical College, Vellore, South India from 1 through 7 September 1995.

We are a group of thirty people from five continents, from Argentina, Brazil, Chile, Costa Rica and Antigua; from Uganda; from Cambodia, India, Philippines and Thailand; from Australia and the United States of America; from Germany, Norway, Sweden, Britain and Ireland. All of us have practical experience in working with church programs related to HIV/AIDS. Some of us are living with HIV/AIDS.

Our task was to share experiences of ongoing work on the theme of "Women and Health and the Challenge of HIV/AIDS." All of us had found that this work had continually challenged our thinking, our attitudes and our theology, and had transformed our vision. In sharing our experiences and the results of our research, we found that we do in fact have much in common; that we gained strength and confidence by exchanging perspectives; and that the issues we faced— though from widely differing contexts—were very much the same. We were able to reach unanimous agreement about an ecumenical platform of action.

## PLATFORM OF ACTION

1. We call upon our churches to engage in self-critical examination of the church's participation in and perpetration of cultural biases and patterns that contribute to women's subordination and oppression.

2. We urge our churches to create an environment where the life experiences of women can be heard without fear of judgment, in an atmosphere of mutual trust and respect, so that the issues that emerge may be addressed.

3. We strongly recommend that the churches re-evaluate the ways in which we have interpreted the Bible, along with church traditions and images of God. Many Christians have

accepted these as truth without considering how far they are (or are not) rooted in people's daily realities, and consistent with the liberating message of Jesus.

4. We challenge the churches to acknowledge openly the sexual dimension of human experience and allow for this dimension to become part of ongoing church dialogue.

5. We commend this platform of action to our churches worldwide in the loving hope that they will remember always, in their consideration, reflection and prayers, that these issues have to do not with abstract ideas but with real people, the quality of their lives, and their well-being and health.

*Vellore, 7 September 1995*

# 1

## WHOLE WOMEN

Do you know what women lack most?
The knowledge, the deep-rooted knowledge and conviction
that they are human beings.

*Fatia Al Assal of Egypt*

### SHUNILA'S STORY

On my office wall hangs a picture. In it, a woman in a sari sits
cross-legged, breastfeeding her baby. Her head is bent in loving
attention, she enfolds the baby in her body's curve so softly that
the two of them look like one—she fulfilled by the baby, the
baby cherished and protected by her. The picture speaks of
nurturing and wholeness, peace and safety. It speaks of the
strength of love. It seems to sum up what we mean when we talk
about wholeness and health.

Made of soft gold straw on a background of scarlet cloth, it's
also a thing of beauty. "I like your Madonna," visitors sometimes
say. "Make a good Christmas card, wouldn't it?"

But this is no Madonna, or at least not in the traditional Christian sense. My picture was made by Shunila from Bangladesh, a
warm, lovely Muslim woman with dark smooth hair and alert eyes,
who organizes the buying of materials for a handicrafts co-oper-
ative that we will call the Jibon (Life) Centre in Dhaka, the capital.

Shunila was born in rural Silhet Province, married at fifteen to
a remote cousin whom she hardly knew, and moved to Dhaka.
On the day her third daughter was born, her husband (who had
another wife anyway) beat her and threw her into the street with
her three little girls and nothing else. She was not quite twenty at
the time.

1

Sick and bleeding, Shunila had nowhere to go. Her family were
unlikely to take her in, even if she'd had the money or the
strength for the journey. A woman rejected by her husband is a
disgrace to the community. She survived on the streets for three
months. It was when the baby, Yami, became desperately ill with
diarrhea that she heard about Jibon, a refuge and day care center
where abandoned, battered or widowed women and their children could get health advice. That was six years ago. It's hard
now to imagine the bedraggled, frightened little family which
must have arrived on the doorstep, or the determination it must
have taken to become what they are today.

Shunila became a member of the group of women who meet
at Jibon. The biggest enemy to health, they recognized, was not
disease but sheer poverty. What was the good of bringing Yami
back from the dead when the family had nowhere to live, no
money to buy food, and no real hope of either? She'd be ill again.
And again. And eventually, sooner rather than later, she'd die.

The women developed a number of small money-making
schemes, and Shunila learned to work with straw, making
colored floor mats. But still children got ill, and medicines were
expensive. At first the project bought these from a local pharmaceutical factory making basic drugs. Then this was closed down,
and they had to use imported drugs at many times the price.
They joined a demonstration against the closure of the factory.
When they came to the center the next morning, they found
their looms had been broken up and their tools stolen.

When Shunila first came to Jibon, one of her ambitions was to
make enough money to allow her to bottlefeed little Yami, which
she'd been told at the hospital was the best way to ensure that
she grew up strong and healthy. But the weekly health education
class at Jibon emphasized the benefits of breastfeeding so
strongly that Shunila was convinced. She now works with a
group, based at Jibon, which is trying to promote breastfeeding
among local women.

This may sound pretty obvious in a country where over 80
percent of people live below the poverty line, and where few
people have clean water for sterilization. But big companies still
encourage poor women to bottlefeed, in spite of the expense.
One afternoon, after Shunila and others had been chatting with
the women waiting in line at the hospital antenatal clinic, some

men followed them down a side street, beat them unconscious, and left them.

And another thing. Shunila has AIDS. She might have got the virus from her husband, who was a truck driver. But then, during the time between leaving her husband's home and arriving at Jibon, trying to keep herself and her children alive, she had a couple of sexual encounters with the men building the new road. They'd paid enough to feed the children for another day. Maybe it was then. She looks back on those times. They had to eat. She'd do the same again. How else could they have survived? She is lucky, she says. She's lucky that she's never been raped, like many of the women who belong to the little group of HIV+ women who meet at Jibon.

But even when she was married, being sexually available was part of the deal, wasn't it? She'd assumed when she got the white discharge that her husband was going with other women; but she laughs gently at the idea that she might have dared refuse him. "At least," she says, "I've got my own work now. Making pictures for a living, I can afford to make my own choices. I don't have to worry about passing the sickness on to other people. And the children do not have the sickness. But it's for them I . . ." She doesn't finish her sentence.

So when I look at my picture, I don't see the sentimental Christmas card scene my visitors see. I see wholeness, yes, and incarnation. But I also see the fragility of that wholeness, and the immense amount of struggle and suffering which—for many of the world's women—goes into maintaining it. I see Shunila. I see three little girls with long, braided hair and shy, wide eyes. In November, I heard that Shunila had died. Her three little girls are effectively orphans. And I wonder what will become of them now.

## What Killed Shunila?

What killed Shunila? Was it, as medical science might tell you, a virus? Was it, as some religious people might say, immorality?

The real problems that faced Shunila were neither medical nor moral ones. They were the whole complex range of factors that govern the infrastructure of many poor women's lives, not just in Bangladesh but within that "Third World" which is woven into the fabric of all societies, rich and poor, in the closing years of

the 20th century. WHO's report *Bridging the Gaps* spells it out
starkly. "For most people in the world today," it says, "every step
of life from infancy to old age is taken under the twin shadows of
poverty and inequity and under the double burden of suffering
and disease."

Shunila was not just desperately poor. She lived in a culture
where women marry young and have little status. She was virtually uneducated, and without marketable skills. She produced girl
children when sons were wanted. The laws failed to prevent her
husband from beating her, and she had no means of claiming a
share of matrimonial property. She was part of a family system
that rejects women who come to grief, without any safety net
within the health and welfare system to compensate; and in
confronting the power of multinational companies, she brought
upon herself the violence that sometimes supports that power.
It's this kind of complex of burdens that provides opportunities,
in the case of so many women, for HIV infection. The most
pressing moral issue for Shunila was to keep her little family alive
for a few more days.

The connection between poverty and ill health cannot be over-
estimated, and, while poverty affects men as well as women, the
heaviest burdens are borne by women. According to *Bridging
the Gaps,* some 1.1 billion people live today in acute poverty, and
the majority of these are women.  The World Bank's report,
published in December 1995, has this to say:

> Doing more to enhance the role and status of women is
> critical to address a wide range of development issues,
> including AIDS. Women must have the power to protect
> themselves—sexually, economically and socially.  For exam-
> ple, a hundred million girls in the developing world never
> get a chance to go to school. Reversing this deplorable situa-
> tion is one of the most effective ways to reduce poverty, and
> also the incidence of all kinds of diseases. And it would help
> empower women to ensure a better future for themselves
> and their families.

But women are not helpless. From all over the world come
stories of the immense effort of growing, getting and preparing
food when there is very little money. WHO estimates that three

out of four households in the developing world have no access to safe drinking water or sanitation. But it is the women who are responsible for carrying water, often many miles a day; and there is evidence that women are particularly susceptible to water-borne disease.

"Women are half the world's population, receive one-tenth of the world's income, account for two-thirds of the world's working hours, and own only one-hundredth of the world's property," says the International Labour Organization. It is often argued that society has provided for this state of affairs by making men responsible for women. An article in *Women in Action* speaks of "the myth of the male provider," a myth that we tend to accept as fact whereas in Latin America, for example, women head over 50 percent of families in some countries and not less than 40 percent in any country. Maybe these figures suggest a deeper truth: that women, given a just society, are perfectly capable of taking responsibility for themselves.

Numerous studies speak of the long hours women work—often 15 hours a day, seven days a week, all the year round—and of this paradoxical fact: that in spite of their contribution to the world's economy in terms of agriculture, trade, child care and domestic labor, the work is invisible. Because they are unpaid, it never appears in the economic figures. There is even growing evidence that, with pressures on the world economy and the continued exodus of men from rural areas to the cities, the gap between women and men, in terms of workload on the one hand and wealth on the other, is getting wider. And not just in the developing world: a recent US study gave evidence that the number of women holding more than one paid job had nearly trebled in the 20 years between 1970 and 1990.

In many societies, sons are seen as a better financial investment than daughters. Sons will ensure the handing-on of property. They will provide financial security for your old age. The birth of girl-babies may therefore be regarded as a matter for commiseration. In India, the large dowries expected from brides when they marry may prove financially devastating to poor families with a number of daughters. In China, one result of the one-child-family laws has been to put a premium on producing a normal, healthy son first time round.

In these countries, technology for determining the sex of a

fetus, combined with the routine use of abortion, makes the womb itself a dangerous place for the girl-child. Sons tend to be welcomed more eagerly when they are born. They are better fed, better educated and they receive better health care than girl-children. Young girls and boys suffer more or less equally from diarrhea, and yet substantially more boys are brought to clinics with the disease. In places where a charge is made for immunization, only about a quarter of children brought for injections are girls.

Boys are better educated, too. And yet there is plenty of evidence that the mother's level of education is the most important factor in determining a family's health (UNFPA, 1989). Lack of education limits choice. In urban areas in particular, the problems facing illiterate women are quite desperate. Scavenging, begging and prostitution may be their only means of surviving. Education, on the other hand, enables women to increase their income, reduce family size, and improve the nutrition level of the whole family. It teaches skills, gives confidence, and provides a springboard into the modern world. And yet in India, where girls are expected to leave home when they marry, twice as many boys enter secondary school; and in Uganda, where all education now has to be paid for, growing girls may be expected to stay at home and care for younger children while their mothers work and their brothers go to school.

Family planning is often spoken of as the key to greater health and prosperity. If family size is uncontrolled, the effects of a heavy workload, poor nutrition, low self-esteem and inadequate housing are multiplied. Yet in many countries, large families are a source of pride. The father proves his manhood, the woman her womanhood, by having children, so that in Africa, for instance, families of ten or more children are not unusual.

Nor are the benefits of planned families universally recognized at government level. In Argentina and Chile, where the Roman Catholic Church has a powerful lobby within government, contraception is not publicly available to poor women, although there are private hospitals and clinics providing it. Illegal backstreet abortions are therefore common.

In many cultures, talk of sexual matters is taboo, and even where this is not strictly the case, there may be no easy way of introducing the subject of contraception. If the woman initiates the conversation, her husband may accuse her of having relationships with other men. The myth that virtuous women must be ignorant in these matters is present in most cultures, although Indian, Thai and Cambodian women suggest that there are particularly powerful taboos in much of Asia. Knowledge about family planning is often hard to get. If girls know too much about sex, the story goes, it will make them promiscuous. And yet every major survey worldwide has shown that the incidence of unintended teenage pregnancy is lowest where sexual matters are most openly discussed.

In recent years, the sale of illegal narcotics has become increasingly commercial and well-organized. Substance abuse has created what can only be described as an international alternative culture, existing within ordinary societies. This is particularly true in Southeast Asia, Latin America and inner-city areas of the USA, in all of which the drug industry goes hand in hand with organized prostitution. While both, today, are multi-million-dollar industries, the chief victims are the poorest people.

It is rarely women who start wars. But almost daily from somewhere in the world comes the media image of a woman crying out in agony. Her home may be gone, her children dead, her husband murdered, her daughter raped. This is the dramatic, public face of the silent scream of women all over the world who are used, abused and violated by men.

**Bob Cowley** is an Australian working with Quaker Peace and Service in Cambodia. Until recently, he was building refugee camps in Bosnia—a big camp for Muslims in Tuzla that the Serbs overran before it was finished, then some refugee "cottages" for Croats on a caravan site in Herzegovina. Now he is back in Cambodia working on a new health center. The rape of women and girls has always been a feature of war, says Bob. But in today's climate of "ethnic cleansing," it seems to have been elevated to a form of warfare in itself, with forced prostitution aimed at defiling communities, humiliating men, and fathering children on the women of the enemy. Women are in the front line. **Terrie Cowley,** Bob's wife, speaks of villages in Bosnia where there are no young women left between the ages of 12 and 22.

The horror still with him, Bob describes the day in Bosnia when he was called to identify the bodies of a murdered family. The father had been crucified. The young girl had been raped, and her eyes gouged out. He talks of the women and children of Cambodia, returning to the "killing fields" where their neighbors and families were murdered by the Khmer Rouge, and then getting blown up or maimed by land mines when they try to farm them. In this situation, health means survival; health means not being murdered. Or not today, anyway.

The creation of migration on a massive scale, and millions of refugees, is a further refinement of 20th-century warfare. The UN High Commissioner for Refugees (UNHCR) estimates that there are 27 million refugees and displaced persons in the world today, most of them women and children, most of them fleeing from war. This implies a breakdown of family and community on an unimaginable scale. In a refugee camp, says Terrie, talk of AIDS is meaningless. There is no future anyway. "Preventive health care" means keeping yourself and your family alive until tomorrow.

Removed from their communities and homes, women and girls are particularly at risk. **Grace Nakazibwe,** whose husband was murdered outside their house in the Ugandan war, speaks of visiting a refugee camp to run a clinic. A woman came up to her and thrust a small girl into her arms. "Please take her," she said. "If she stays here she'll be raped before she's twelve." Then she disappeared into the crowd. This child is now nineteen. Neither she nor Grace has ever seen the mother again.

The high rate of HIV infection in refugee camps is becoming a matter of great concern. HIV flourishes, particularly, in situations of hopelessness and social breakdown. HIV control demands a measure of control over one's own life, a sense of self, of self-worth, and a belief that there is a future which is worth planning for. In a refugee camp, women and children have none of these.

## WHAT GIVES WOMEN AIDS?

Reversing economic, social and political biases against women is often presented primarily as a moral or human rights issue. As the above pages may suggest, it is becoming an issue of survival. "In the context of AIDS," said Jonathan Mann, when he was director of WHO's Global AIDS program, "the subordination of women has become an urgent threat to public health."

In Europe, the USA and in most of Latin America, most people still work on the assumption that HIV is an epidemic of homosexual men, or of intravenous drug injectors and their partners.

This is no longer the case. There is a clear rise in the proportion of women infected. While figures are constantly going out of date, estimates as I write suggest that the actual figures for HIV infection are around 8.5 men to one woman in North America, 2:1 in Southeast Asia, and in parts of Sub-Saharan Africa women are said to be in the majority. The proportion of women to men infected with the virus is going up everywhere, and WHO believes that by the turn of the century, worldwide, the number of seropositive women and men will be equal. And while infection via drug injection and blood transfusion occur, the huge majority of HIV+ women have contracted the virus through heterosexual intercourse, most of them with their spouses.

As a result of the largely male profile of the infection in Europe and North America, though, most of the research has been done either on HIV as it affects men, or on factors governing mother-to-fetus transmission. As a result, less information is available about its effects on women, so that early signs of infection (which are not the same in women as in men) are less likely to be detected. Participants in drug trials, too, are commonly—sometimes entirely—male, so that treatments for women are less well developed.

Women are biologically more vulnerable than men to all sexually transmitted diseases. The likelihood of their becoming infected with HIV as a result of a single sexual encounter is nearly three times that of a heterosexual male. There is a 25 percent chance of a man catching gonorrhea from unprotected sex with an infected woman, a 50 percent chance of a woman catching it from an infected man. This is because the concentration of virus or bacteria in semen is far greater than it is in the vaginal secretions of the woman, and the vaginal membranes are more permeable than the surface of the penis. They are also more subject to injury. Rape, forced sex or the presence of other sexually transmitted disease greatly increases the likelihood of infection by providing open sores or lacerations that allow the virus to enter the bloodstream.

This biological vulnerability is often reinforced by cultural, social and economic factors, many of them outlined above, that limit women's ability to protect themselves from infection. Women may want to stipulate fidelity, safe sex, or no sex at all, but where society defines the male partner's needs as paramount, it's very difficult for women to negotiate strategies to protect their health. Ugandan M.P. Miria Matembe says, "The women tell us they see their husbands with the wives of men who have died of AIDS. And they ask, 'What can we do? If we say no, they'll say we must pack up and go. But if we do, where do we go to?' They are dependent on the men and they have nowhere to go" (*Panos, 1990*).

Asked what advice he would give to heads of state as being the most effective single policy for dealing with HIV/AIDS, Jonathan Mann suggests reform of the legal apparatus to strengthen a woman's right to negotiate safe sex with her partner. But for that you need to live in a stable society with enforceable laws, a legal system accessible to everyone, and support at family and community levels for the provisions of the law. Few societies fill that bill. Over most of the globe, the gap between rich and poor is growing. HIV infection must be seen in the context of increasingly powerful global factors such as debt, international trading practices, an aggressive arms trade whose very existence promotes war and its attendant social chaos. The effect of the global economy has been to create ghettoes of "untouchables" within all societies. These groups and individuals benefit very little from laws, and are, increasingly, structurally excluded from the benefits of prosperity. A world that condones this situation is neither just nor safe. It is in this international context that the experiences described in the following chapters should be understood.

# 2

# AFRICAN SPRING

## THE PEARL OF AFRICA

Returning to Africa is always an emotional experience for me. I spent much of my childhood in Southern Africa and, as a young woman, worked for a while at Korle Bu Hospital in Accra, Ghana. I've always longed to come to Uganda, though. And I've come determined to follow the instructions of my Ugandan colleagues James Oporiah-Ekwaro and Eva Kisitu. "You'll find lots of problems," they said, "but make sure you see the wonderful things as well, the things Ugandans are proud of."

It's not usually the wonderful things about Uganda that appear in the world press. Which is a pity, because it's a beautiful country, christened "the pearl of Africa" by Winston Churchill. Uganda has transformed itself since January 1986, when the National Resistance Army entered Kampala, ending the extreme violence of the Amin and Obote decades, and bringing President Yoweri Museveni to power. Yet it's still a desperately poor country, committed to debt repayments running to 60 percent of its foreign exchange earnings—three times the International Monetary Fund's estimate for sustainability.

Life expectancy, at 42 years, is the lowest in the world. This is largely due to AIDS. Ugandan government figures indicate that around 1.5 million Ugandans are HIV-positive—just under 10 percent of the population. However, testing of pregnant women suggests that HIV affects between 10 and 20 percent of the population in Entebbe, and 20 to 30 percent in Kampala, while a Medical Research Council study showed that 50 percent of people in one trading center on the trans-Africa highway in south-western Uganda were infected. The town's bars and discos,

11

cheap lodging houses and brothels make it a popular overnight stop for truckers; some blame centers such as this for the speed with which the virus has spread through Sub-Saharan Africa.

Coffin makers are having a field day, though. Undertakers advertise on the roadsides, and everywhere you will see cyclists wobbling along with long black boxes strapped to the backs of their bikes. Death is ever-present, and you can't avoid knowing it. It's how you respond to that knowledge that matters.

From WHO, however, there is some evidence that the rate of new infections is leveling off. It's difficult to say whether this is due to a real change in behavior—fewer partners, for instance, or more widespread use of condoms. But there are posters everywhere, on tree trunks and walls and hoardings. Explicit advice is offered on radio and in the newspapers. It's impossible to avoid being aware of AIDS. "Ugandans look at AIDS as very much their problem," says epidemiologist Jane Kengeya. "Awareness is very high, even in the poorest rural areas. . . . Ugandans no longer look at death as someone else's problem." It appears that Uganda's openness about AIDS, in contrast to the culture of denial which exists in some other countries, may be starting to pay off.

I am met by Sam Mabirizi, driver from the Uganda Protestant Medical Bureau, coordinator of the Participatory Action Research program in Uganda. We drive along the lakeshore, and there on the hillside is Kampala: in the mist, an extraordinary modern city rising from the shacks and markets and red earth of Africa. Does Sam think Museveni has done well? Yes. The people trust him. There is peace. People are building houses, buying cars. There is confidence. He is not right about everything, but then who is?

And Kampala, for all the country's poverty and political uncertainty, seems, when we get there, so safe and normal and friendly. Or the people do. But that distant panorama of towers soaring into the morning mist belies the real state of this city, which is painfully battered and run down. It's sad, because Kampala is a beautiful place—a city set on seven hills, with stunning buildings, flame trees in full flower, cafes and markets humming, people sitting in the parks reading and playing with children. But broken-down, burned-out, shell-holed, peeling buildings are everywhere, the roads are all potholed and muddy. So many things got damaged in the war, and the government has a massive job on hand to make it lovely again.

## DOES THIS COUNT AS HEALING?

Mengo-Kisenyi is a Kampala slum area. Jane's father, Philip Kisogi, is chairman of one of the health committees. The family lives in a house on the main street, with its own pineapple, banana, sugar cane and *matooke* stall outside. The family currently consists of Philip and Joyce Kisogi and their three younger children; five grandchildren, the orphans of their elder daughter, who died of AIDS earlier in the year; Jane's two children, one of them an HIV+ baby, who are currently staying with other relatives; and Jane herself, who is dying of AIDS. Her husband is "sick" too, but his family sent her home to her own parents when she became too ill to care for him.

On the wall there is a picture of them both, happy and prosperous, as they once were. Now she lies on a mattress on the floor, with her face turned to the wall. She has diarrhea. She can't eat because the thrush in her mouth makes it difficult to swallow, and she vomits up what she is given. But she turns on the bed when she hears Jessica's voice, and smiles weakly.

I am traveling, in Uganda, with **Erlinda Senturias,** the Filipina doctor who co-ordinates the WCC's AIDS program. We are visiting this house with Jessica Abisa and Imelda Bulwadela, from the primary health center at St. John's Mission in Mengo-Kisenyi. We crowd in and sit down. Joyce Kisogi is a tall, dignified, good-looking woman, but propped, now, against the door frame, looking exhausted. Other sisters arrive, and younger children.

How to make Jane more comfortable? "You must eat," says her mother. But no drugs are available to stop the vomiting. The primary health center can afford only the most basic drugs and vaccines. Eventually, from her handbag, Erlinda produces some anti-histamine pills she takes herself to stop side-effects from anti-malarial drugs. High-tech medicine it is not, but this half-hour represents a real corporate effort to sustain the family and lend some dignity to the dying woman. Does this count as healing? Helping people to die with dignity?

Five years ago, Mengo-Kisenyi was filthy and dangerous and swarming with mosquitoes. Today it is still terribly poor, with high rents and whole families living in a space not much bigger than our London bathroom, virtually all of it taken up by a curtained-off bed. But the zone we are in is generally clean and it does have an air of organization. This is said to be at least partly thanks to **Rebecca Wasswa** and Jessica, who run the primary health service at St. John's Mission, and who have set up a health committee as an adjunct to the local government Resistance Committee. By going into the community and looking after sick people, and helping families to do the same, says Philip Kisogi, the St. John's people have transformed the area and given people hope and a sense of purpose.

The community has an unusually high proportion of people with HIV/AIDS, who five years ago would have kept quiet about their sickness and lived "normal" lives till they became too ill to hide it. Today, there is less of a culture of denial. But, people say, it's still impossible to change your sexual habits overnight when you discover you are HIV+. Because if you suddenly stop having sex, or insist on using a condom, everyone will guess why. Then you run the risk of losing your job, and being abandoned by your family and left to die.

Our next call is on Rose, who lives with the virus and four children. She is holding Soffia, who is a pretty, lively, two-year-old. Rose's husband died of AIDS a couple of years back, leaving three wives and seven other children. He didn't have much to leave, and by the time it was divided, Rose was left with two chairs and a mattress. Soffia and the third child are both HIV+. The second has sickle cell anemia. Only the eldest is likely to live long.

Rose was once a typist for the ministry of labor, but was made redundant shortly after she was diagnosed as HIV+. She misses the company and the work as much as she misses the money. She's lucky though: her house belongs to her own family, and the eldest child is being educated by her brother, who is a doctor. She has enjoyed meeting us: her English is good, and she likes having someone to talk to.

Then through the narrow red lanes, tripping over scraggy toddlers in filthy, ankle-length adult T-shirts, and we come to a little clearing with plants to one side, and behind them a slightly larger house—the home of an AIDS widow who has started a women's income-generating project there.

A week later, at the end of our visit to Uganda, we return to Mengo-Kisenyi. They are preparing for two AIDS funerals—one of the ragged urchins, and Jane. Jane died on the day after our visit. She asked for some milk; they gave it to her; she smiled and went to sleep. And that was it. Her parents now have ten children to look after—three of their own and two families of orphaned grandchildren.

## GRASPING THE NETTLE

The figures for HIV infection in Uganda are among the highest in the world. Infection is most prevalent in the most economically productive age-groups. The illness and death of so many young adults has placed immense stresses on communities, and resulted in hundreds of thousands of widows and orphans, many of them HIV-infected themselves, many of them completely destitute. With so many of the youth unemployed and no free schooling, the spread of the virus among young people with nothing much to do and no hope of a better life is a matter of great concern.

In a country with very limited material resources to spend on health care, this is not primarily an issue for the medical profession. It is a challenge to communities, and it is a challenge to a context in which economic factors and imported patterns of entertainment and consumption combine with traditional cultural ways of life to encourage the spread of HIV.

While government and other educational programs have been relatively successful in helping people to understand the facts about AIDS (a survey conducted in 1995 showed that around 85 percent knew how to recognize it and how it is spread), there is little sign that people's behavior has altered. Traditional approaches to sexuality and to personal relationships are too deeply rooted for education programs devised by professionals from outside the community to be effective in producing change.

Community development methodologies have also failed to deal with the issue of HIV. The private and intimate nature of the activities involved, and the assumptions about individual, community and cultural identity in which they are rooted, make problem-solving, outcome-oriented methodologies unacceptable.

The idea for Participatory Action Research (PAR) arose from the perception that communities so burdened with the problems produced by HIV are: (a) in urgent need of building up their capacity for coping; and (b) strongly motivated towards a fundamental examination of cultural and other issues that reduce that capacity. Current educational and development methodologies may be inappropriate for encouraging this. What was needed was for communities to be enabled to do their own research, to identify the issues that need to be addressed, and to develop strategies for dealing with those issues.

In 1991, at a WCC workshop in Nairobi, it was decided to try this in a few places in Tanzania, Uganda and Zaire. Participating agencies were the three national church-related health co-ordinating agencies—the Christian Medical Board of Tanzania, the Uganda Protestant Medical Bureau, and the Church of Christ in Zaire.

Professional researchers coming from a traditional academic culture are often uncomfortable with Participatory Action Research. Usually, a researcher sets objectives and decides on the questions to be answered. Data is then compiled and analyzed, and a report drawn up. This is sent to concerned professionals, and also, possibly, to the research population.

Not so with PAR. Here, the research facilitator and the population decide jointly on the research objectives, the facilitator's role being to prompt critical thinking rather than to set directions. The research population then reflects on its own practices, either in identity groups (e.g., young men, mothers, people with AIDS) or in mixed groups reflecting the make-up of the community. They define the problem, propose solutions, plan for action, and suggest ways of monitoring results.

If PAR is to succeed, it is vital that the entry point be recognized as a burning issue by the community involved. In the countries participating in this program, HIV infection is an issue of this magnitude. The number of deaths has reached crisis level, predominantly among young people, and in women and men in the most economically productive age-groups, many of them parents of young families. Families and communities are often reeling under the responsibility of caring for orphans. A Zairean study suggested that by the year 2000 there would be three-quarters of a million AIDS orphans in Zaire alone.

The PAR program has identified some factors that encourage transmission of the virus: poverty and the low self-esteem that accompanies it; lack of meaningful information, compounded by some traditional beliefs and by conflicting media reports; the attraction of western lifestyles and entertainment; the situation of young people; traditional expectations about women; and the popularity of all-night celebrations, particularly when accompanied by alcohol.

Information first. However carefully public education campaigns are designed, they will be effective only if they carry more conviction than existing assumptions. It's easy for people to avoid acting on new information if their belief in sorcery and religious healing is deeper than their belief in the source of the education. It confuses them if they read in the press one day that HIV causes AIDS and the next day that it doesn't, and it gives them permission to assume that it's all nonsense anyway. If you've grown up believing that intercourse with young girls or boys or with older men and women is a guarantee against sexually transmitted diseases, then you are likely to graft that belief onto the new understandings. If most people—as the Zairean PAR suggests—see education mainly as "being told what to do," then they may be inclined to reject it entirely.

Cultural changes resulting from exposure to western ways of life were also blamed. The Tanzanian study was especially vehement about this. Young people in particular are influenced by what they see on TV and video, and attracted by discos and consumer goods. The fragmentation of extended families into smaller "nuclear" units was seen as destroying the network of influences through which children are prepared for sexual experience. In any case, there are taboos around discussing sex within the family. There was universal concern about the dangers to young people, particularly those to which young men without skills or hope of employment are exposed. Many have no sense of a life-project, no real prospect of getting together the money needed for marriage and children. This "prolonged bachelor lifestyle" is seen as leading to idleness, to indiscriminate sex and even to rape. Low self-esteem, accompanied by a "don't care attitude," is a particular problem in this group.

Blame is placed on celebrations, traditional rites and parties, particularly those that go on all night, and that may habitually culminate in sexual activity. Some groups mentioned the evening prayer meetings organized by the local churches as examples. The danger is aggravated by the availability of alcohol, which was generally recognized as contributing to uncontrolled sexual behavior.

But by far the largest group of factors were those connected to the situation of women. Poverty, generally seen as the main factor encouraging transmission, presents particular dangers to women. Sex may be regarded as a way of paying for goods. "HIV kills in three to ten years; hunger kills in three days. I have three children. Why should we starve if I can get money for immediate use?" Sugar daddies may offer a solution, and are often the only way young girls can afford an education. The fact that women's work is so often unpaid, and the entire property of the marriage is assumed to belong to the man, means that women do not have, within marriage, the power to make choices.

These are almost universal factors in transmission. In the countries studied, they are compounded by particular cultural traditions. The pride taken in large families is incompatible with condom use within marriage. The practice of women walking long distances for water or firewood, often alone and in the dark, is seen as an opportunity for casual adultery or rape. Widow inheritance by a dead husband's brother is a high risk practice. Polygamy is common in all these countries, so that an infected man may pass on HIV to a number of women and then, by vertical transmission, to their babies. Traditionally, the husband's clan inherits property, so that the dead man's wives and children may then be thrown out on the street.

And finally, there is the church. People spoke of moralistic attitudes among clergy, and the stigmatization of people with AIDS. They talked about the need for churches to be "honest about realities" in terms of sexual matters, particularly with young people, and to face up to a dualism between spiritual life and sexuality in much church teaching.

It is impossible here to report fully on the findings of this ambitious and wide-ranging study. The above remarks are intended only as an insight into the most commonly mentioned factors in transmission. A sample selection of the kinds of action taken within particular communities as a result of PAR is listed on page 19.

The participating agencies in Zaire, Tanzania and Uganda find the Participatory Action Research program very significant. Many of the factors held to be responsible for HIV transmission (including poverty, lack of training for youth, the precarious status of women before the law) have been condemned already by physicians, development workers, politicians and churches on

## COMMUNITY ACTION TAKEN AS A RESULT OF PAR

- Moves to ban the practice of widows being inherited by male relatives.

- Encouraging men to make sensible wills, leaving property to their own wives and children.

- Clan leaders insisting that couples who are to marry are tested for HIV before cultural introductions are carried out.

- Special educational clan meetings for young people, to help them evaluate cultural practices, and to persuade them to observe restrictions on discos, bars, and traditional all-night dance ceremonies.

- Asking clients to bring their own razor blades when a traditional healer is consulted.

- Efforts to integrate traditional understandings of healing with scientific medical ones.

- Traditional healers agreeing to employ both sexes in clinics, so that patients may be treated by someone of the same sex. This minimizes the practice of the healer having sexual intercourse with the patient.

- Rubbing herbal medicines on instead of cutting the skin.

- Limiting, controlling or abolishing all-night celebrations and closing discos at 10 p.m. .

- Clan leaders recommending that where traditional ceremonies must continue through the night, both partners be there to police each other.

- Attempts to limit drinking hours.

- Men escorting their wives to collect firewood or water at night, or women walking in groups, or, sometimes, men doing these jobs instead of the women.

the grounds that they are socially inequitable and act as barriers to development. Now a study carried out by the people concerned addresses an issue that they themselves believe to be a matter of life and death, and what happens? These very factors are identified as the culprits in the transmission of HIV, and the challenges implicit in the subordinate position of women are judged the most intractable of all.

## KAGOMA AND THE "GENDER BALANCE MOVEMENT"

Kagoma is about 20 minutes drive from Jinja, site of the source of the Nile and a major marketing center for southern Uganda. This area is greener and more fertile that Kampala. All Saints Health Centre is up a long, rutted, red dirt road, between mealie fields and banana trees. As we turn down towards the main clinic building, the jeep is surrounded by the fluttering hands of dancing, ululating women. The chairwomen and -men of nine of the twelve local committees are there, with women's leaders, trainers, and trainers' trainers. The place is packed. We are warmly greeted by **Christopher Tusubira,** social research co-ordinator and program manager. People make speeches. Even I make a speech. Erlinda teaches everyone a Filipino song.

Kagoma was one of the pilot areas for the Uganda Protestant Medical Bureau's Participatory Action Research into the root causes of HIV transmission. Observing how many of the entry points identified were connected with the roles and status of women in their communities, All Saints Health Centre decided to set up a satellite research program in which the population studied their own way of life, identifying the windows of transmission for HIV as they relate specifically to the balance of power between men and women, and exploring ways in which these windows might be closed. Examples of issues identified in these discussions are listed on pages 21-22.

The work was undertaken by women and men with the involvement of community leaders and the consent of the whole community. An estimated 17 percent of all people in the area are HIV-positive, though of course the percentage is lower among children and old people, and much higher among young people and economically productive men and women. Every village has its AIDS orphans, many of them infected themselves. It's this crisis which lends such urgency to the work, and has brought

### Risk Factors for Women Identified in the Course of PAR

- Lack of economic opportunities for women, resulting in dependence on men for support.

- The practice of widows being inherited by male relatives.

- Polygamous marriages.

- The need for large families.

- Inheritance practices, by which property reverts to the husband's family.

- Cultural and moral attitudes to sexuality.

- Women walking alone, sometimes long distances and in the dark, to fetch water or collect firewood.

- Western cultural influences, including discos, uncensored film shows and marriages outside the traditional framework, all of which interfere with the traditional community checks and balances.

- Resistance to pre-marriage HIV-testing.

- Sexual favors in return for money or goods—an insoluble problem unless women's economic position improves.

- Resistance within families to sex education for children, many of whom start having sex before the age of ten.

- Illiteracy, ignorance of legal rights.

- The idea that "real men" have irresistible sexual urges that can only be satisfied by full sexual intercourse.

- Acceptance of the practice of men bringing other women into the home at night.

- Labor migration, where the man is away for eleven months out of twelve.

- Strong cultural resistance to condom use.

- Most women's dislike of condoms.

- Associating condoms with promiscuity.

> - The view that "AIDS touches an activity that is impossible to stop; only a virgin will be saved."
> - Male alcoholism.
> - All-night ceremonies.

together people who ten years ago would never have dreamed that they would be working for change in a patriarchal system that goes back hundreds of years. "But it's not just the women who are dying," said one man. "It's our brothers, and our sons and grandsons. We could give up and say 'everyone is dead,' but then we will never change this. We have to say 'everyone is alive, and we must make sure they stay alive.' This is too important to leave to the women."

Nevertheless, in terms of "actors" in the community who need to be involved, women and girl children are identified as the primary group. They are the ones who are most acutely caught up in the conditions (some of which were identified above) that lead to transmission, and their perceptions and suggestions are crucial. Men are the secondary audience, although, says Christopher Tusubira, it is at this level that the final power to effect or sanction change is situated.

The tertiary audience consists of elderly men and women. These have been described as "cultural traditionalist hard-liners," and it is here that the real bedrock of tradition is located in terms of the dissemination of cultural beliefs, myths, superstitions and popular legends. This group consists of people who were themselves denied basic rights, and grew up believing that this was the right and proper way for things to be. This is a crucial group because they are likely to put up the strongest resistance to change. Tusubira believes that 65 percent of gender issues are brewed up at this level.

Imagine rural Africa: extreme poverty, huts in ruins, children everywhere; and then the incredible generosity of nature which allows a broken shack to be showered with bougainvillea, a gutted slum with blossom. We sit under a tree for a whole sun-drenched afternoon, while a group of women reflect on the lack of economic power that makes them so dependent.

Traditionally, domestic livestock are the husband's property. It is the women's job to look after the goats and chickens, but the husband decides when they are to be killed or taken to market, and he gets the proceeds when they are sold. So the women, however hard they work, are unable to make any money for themselves, nor do they have the freedom to undertake other economically productive work.

The first step towards independence is to make some money of your own. Through small-scale income-generating schemes, backed up by saving schemes that offer low-interest loan facilities, Kagoma women have been able to buy their own animals, sell them when they want to, and thus build up credits in the bank. They speak of the men's initial surprise, and then the changed relationships caused not just by the men's realization that their wives are able to make money on their own, but also from the sense of self-worth the women have acquired themselves.

When a couple marries, it's the husband's responsibility to provide beds and bedding. This is no good, say the women. The man can ask you to leave the bed if he is not satisfied. It makes him feel he is free to bring other women to the house, to share "his" bed. So a group of women set up a bedding fund, out of which they bought their own beds and bedding. "Now that this is my bed," said one woman, "I feel I can control what happens in it."

They turn to the subject of domestic violence. In the huddle of small huts that make up their village, you can always hear when a woman is being beaten. In the old days, they used to shut their ears and pretend not to hear; traditionally, you don't interfere between a husband and wife. Today, if they hear these sounds, the community has decreed that other villagers should go out and bang on the walls of the house until the beating stops.

There are older women in the group, but only one of them speaks. A few men wander in and sit listening. "It's not just the women who decided this, you know," says one man fiercely. "We have all decided. Men cannot stop Slim (AIDS) on their own. The women must learn to help."

"But it's better like this anyway," says another.

The conversation drifts to property law, the problems of polygamy, the importance of husbands making proper wills in favor of their wives, the dilemma surrounding the inheritance of widows. If your man gets sick and dies, you may be left with nothing. But if the community says you are not to be given to your brother-in-law, then the community must find other ways of helping you survive.

The talking goes on, and the sun rides across the sky. One by one, we shift between the trees, looking for new patches of shade. Children grizzle or huddle comatose on their mothers' laps. People sleep and wake, come and go, and the mosquitoes crystallize out of the dying light. I am overcome by the parallels with the feeding of the 5000.

Afterwards, we trudge back to the clinic and collapse, with staff, over cups of tea. **Florence Nali** is a community health researcher, and chair of the Gender Balance Group. Florence herself has AIDS; her husband died of it two years ago, and now she is often sick. "Women are brought up in a culture where they're regarded as inferior," she says. "They need encouraging. They need to learn to say to each other, 'Don't go out alone; talk to your husband.'"

HIV has highlighted the need for the emancipation of women with AIDS so that they can look after themselves and believe in the future, and don't spread the virus to others. "But men are changing all the time, too," says Florence. "They're changing because of women."

"That's true," says Christopher. "Men can change. After all, who is dying? Whose daughters are being raped? Who is going to get sick? But the community must be very clear in identifying its mission statement, so everyone understands what the vision is. And it's absolutely crucial that men and women agree together about it."

Food appears: rice and chicken and beef and vegetables and *muzungu* potatoes, and mangoes and pineapple and papaya. We sit around on benches, chatting quietly. Then it is time to go. *Chirungi,* we say. *Chirungi nyo* (thanks very much). And stumble back home to Jinja.

I lie in bed for a long time waiting for sleep. Then somewhere over the Nile water, a baby wails. A picture from this morning comes into my mind—twenty-odd tiny children singing songs, a nursery for AIDS orphans, those most pitiful victims of the HIV pandemic. Their parents dead, these tiny children have been taken in by grandparents too old to cope, by relatives who are already burdened with numerous children of their own, by strangers in whose homes they have become little more than slaves. At the local school, a specially appointed senior teacher is employed full-time to provide basic parenting for older children whose parents have died of AIDS.

The building used for the nursery was given by a local widow, who helps run it. Many of the children, when they first came, were filthy, covered in lice, and grossly underweight. For us, they sing. But it's one of these children I think of now, crouching in the corner sucking his thumb, his eyes glazed. They think he is about four but he has never spoken, will not feed himself, just sits staring into space. As I drift into an exhausted sleep, it's these blank eyes that are etched on the retina of my mind.

## PICNIC TIME

Morning dawns, heavy with rain. We all have headaches. We arrive at Kagoma as the people are gathering for the Sunday morning service. It's worth getting there early, because the clinic at Kagoma doubles as a meeting room and church, and at least two-thirds of the congregation have to sit outside. Today there are fewer people than usual; there have been four AIDS deaths this week, and families are away mourning or preparing for funerals.

As the service opens, the heavens open. Torrents of rain hit the iron roof, and the thunder rolls. "A blessing," people say doubtfully. It takes some 15 minutes for those sitting outside to wedge themselves under cover—on top of each other on the floor and passage, hanging onto the windows, perched all over the consulting rooms.

During the service, the thunder rumbles off into the distance, the rain quietens, and a hot sun appears. The ground steams. Emerging, blinking, people eat their picnics, and then the real business of the day begins: a pageant of presentations from local groups on AIDS and HIV. In that rural place there is an extraordinary amount of talent. Almost all the participants are HIV+, notably the Kagoma women's health education group, who present a half-hour drama with a complicated story involving an innocent wife, an unfaithful husband, a commercial sex worker, a girl student, a sugar daddy, a traditional healer with a multi-purpose, unsterilized razor blade. As a result of a network of infection, absolutely everyone in this story ends up HIV-positive. But the highlight of the afternoon is a truly remarkable group of young people called Mutai Kange. They sing songs they have written themselves, and act out dramas that they perform with mime and dance and drums and with passionate energy in the hot sunshine.

The audience—hundreds of them—are spellbound. Young men perch on top of antheaps or up trees, small children sprawl in front, round-eyed with attention. It is all acted out with such intelligence and humor, such joy in movement and rhythm, such delight in sexuality, that the audience is rolling in the grass with laughter, and it is impossible to believe that every single one of the actors is "sick."

We finish before dark. These big celebrations can easily go on into the night, until the controlled ritual of the dance breaks down, and what is funny and joyful turns into a quite aggressive sexuality, potentially uncontrolled. For this reason, local commit-tees in some areas have tried to control HIV by banning all meet-ings, even prayer meetings, that take place after dark.

People pile onto the waiting truck, then off it, then on again; off—on, off—on, it's not clear why. Many songs and farewells later, we are suddenly in our own van, and the whole convoy lumbers off down the rough track and onto the rutted road. The lorry goes first, carrying Mutai Kange still hard at it on the drums, then a groaning pick-up truck, then us. One by one, still singing, the convoy drops people off at their homes, until finally we're down to around twenty, jolting, hot and happy, through the night to Jinja.

At the Sunset Hotel, a long table is set out on the terrace. "Soda" and roasted groundnuts come. Sam, our driver, seems somehow to have acquired a baby in the course of the day, and he nurses it dreamily. The moon is sickle-shaped, earth-red, and haloed with mist. The Nile gleams in the gathering night. As we watch, the dusk thickens and the sun sets in great scarlet paintbrushfuls over the black water. By the time the Kagoma party leaves, the African moon has risen out of the hills and taken its peaceful place in the star-filled sky.

I sit and take it all in for a while, then go to bed.

## "AFRICA CANNOT BE QUARANTINED"

I am a product of my own culture. When the principles of the "gender balance movement" were explained to me, I assumed (though I was too polite to say so) that this was basically feminism with a fancy name.

This view is quite passionately rejected by **Grace Nakazibwe,** who runs the community-based health program for the Uganda Protestant Medical Bureau. Western feminism with its confrontational style will never make headway in Ugandan society. She doesn't know about the rest of the world, but here relationships between men and women lie at the very heart of the culture. Shifts in the balance of power between them are impossible without the agreement of both. Lasting change can only be negotiated if it's seen to benefit the whole community.

In Uganda, HIV has burst upon communities, and is forcing their members to respond. But the great strength of the Participatory Action Research process is that it really does show where change needs to occur if ways forward are to be found. The language of "rights" is inappropriate here, says Grace. It would inject adversarial elements into the debate, and could only alienate and threaten men and young people who have not so far perceived what is happening in those terms. It would also sabotage a successful indigenous movement, which the people have claimed as their own, by redefining it according to western cultural standards. It would be a lie.

One of the challenges which has come from the experience of HIV is to empower women and girls so that they are able to participate in the survival of their own families and communities. This is a matter of overriding importance to men and women, and also to young people. It's not a matter of rights, says Grace, it's a matter of *survival.* It's not to do with justice, it's to do with *life.*

But it's not just my western feminist view of "rights" that is challenged. It's also my view of what constitutes education. Most people in Uganda know how HIV is transmitted, and what it is like to die of AIDS. It's impossible to avoid this knowledge. But just knowing something doesn't mean you can do anything about it. The billboards tell you to abstain, be monogamous, use a condom. Your head tells you this is right; but the entire fabric of the culture into which your own life is woven says it's impossible. As one woman put it, "AIDS touches an activity that is impossible to stop; only a virgin will be saved."

First, true information is essential. But changing behavior is not just a matter of knowing facts. If those facts are threatening or unpleasant, the temptation will be to hide from them, to summon up all the evidence you can find that might prove they are not, after all, true. If I don't open the envelope containing my bank statement, I can go on pretending I haven't got an overdraft, and then I won't have to change my spending habits. Until I face the truth, I'll never do anything about it.

In a traditional society in particular, behavior change may well be something you can't do on your own at all, and I am convinced that, for all our self-confident individualism, this is equally true for western cultures. Our behavior is dictated by tradition, by habit, by the expectations and lifestyle and values of those around us. Cultures don't change unless they're forced to, either by events from outside or by the threat of self-destruction from within. And before you can change, you have to face the truth.

The programs I have described in this chapter are examples of what people can achieve when they turn and face the threat, search for truth, and then have the courage to act on it. But that's not the end of the story. The explosion of HIV in Sub-Saharan Africa is not just a matter of concern for Africans. Zimbabwe's health minister, Timothy Stamps, says this:

> The world tends to forget that although Africa is an artificial island by virtue of the Suez Canal, it cannot be made into an artificial island of HIV; that will affect people in the rest of the world by virtue of increased mobility, availability of travel, tourism and so forth, which will increase the risk to all people. There is some perverse sense that Africa has had it, in terms of HIV infection and other economic conditions, but there will be problems for those countries who believe we can somehow be quarantined.

HIV is the product of poverty, of marginalization, of disempowerment, of hopelessness. But it's not just women, not just local communities who are poor, marginalized, hopeless or disempowered. On the world stage, the poverty of Africa is coming to be taken for granted, the stranglehold of debt and other global economic factors accepted as facts of life that can't be changed. More consumed than consumer as a result of its colonial history and its present struggles, Africa as a whole becomes more and more marginalized from a world increasingly ruled by market forces. This state of affairs is beginning to look as if it were somehow inevitable—not just that Africa is powerless to do anything about it, but that the rest of world is too.

In Uganda itself, for all its poverty, there is a sense of hope. But there is crushing and dreadful poverty as well; in a country which desperately needs skills, a generation of children is growing up with no free schooling, while 60 percent of the country's earnings go to pay the debt. There may not be hopelessness, but there is anger. And there is AIDS. As Dr. Stamps said, Africa cannot be quarantined.

# 3

# HIS AND HERS:
# A NOTE ON GENDER ANALYSIS

## WHAT ABOUT THE WOMEN?

What are the first questions most people ask about a newborn baby? They'll want to know if it's a healthy child, of course. But before that, usually, they'll ask if the baby is a boy or a girl. In English, we can't, grammatically, refer to the baby as a human being at all without using either its name or a pronoun that labels "it" as female or male. Girl or boy—this is considered to be *the* most important thing about the new person's identity, the thing that, more than anything else, will govern his or her whole future.

This isn't just because of the biological differences that govern the contribution each will make to the reproductive process— what, in English, we would describe as the child's *sexual* characteristics. The meaning I attach to "being a woman," the meaning my brother attaches to "being a man" is deeply ingrained in our identities and in our sense of what it means to belong to our own society. From the moment of birth, we started to learn these rules and conventions so that, as we grew up, we internalized the expectations other people had of us as male and female people, learned to judge ourselves according to them, and to see our own future roles in society reflected in them.

It's this structuring of people's roles, in the family and in society at large, in accordance with what's expected of them as male and female people, that we now define as **gender.** My biological identity determines whether I can give birth to children, but not whether I look after them, or cook the meals.

Gender also determines who owns or has access to what (e.g., land or money), who runs things (e.g., banks or governments), who has what rights and what responsibilities (e.g., caring for sick family members or going out at night with friends). It governs the way I relate to other people. Our biological differences are given; our gender differences are learned, and can therefore be unlearned. Becoming "gender-aware" involves becoming conscious of how this works.

Learned or not, the really interesting thing is how *natural* the gender arrangements seem when you look at your own society. I take it for granted that I can choose my own husband, own a car, go into a bar on my own, sit down to eat with men, take an equal part in decisions about the children, and that, if my husband dies before I do, I will inherit the matrimonial home. This seems natural to me, and also right. There is less agreement about such things as women being managing directors, bishops or airline pilots, which are less familiar roles for women in my society. There is no biological reason why a woman shouldn't do these things, or indeed why a man should not stay at home and look after the children. And yet in my culture—and even more so in cultures with more rigid gender role assumptions—a woman doing these things is likely to run into relationship difficulties.

If the way men and women interrelate is "part of a natural order," it's only a short step to believing that God has ordained that it should be like this. Which is why, in almost all societies, relations between women and men are regarded as a theological issue, and religious institutions and their hierarchies have been some of the most intractable opponents of change.

There is almost no society on earth where you can become "gender-aware" without reaching two conclusions: first, that women are less socially privileged than men; and second, that men are the ones with the economic, political and commercial power.

At first, feminists tended to assume that this was a specifically *women's* problem. If women were consulted about matters that affected them, encouraged to increase their income, form co-operatives, work together with other women to improve their own lives and those of their families, then the rest would follow. Inequality could be addressed by legislating to allow women economic and political rights and access to professions, and by helping them get the education that would enable them to take advantage of these new opportunities.

The "women's issue" approach is essential to creating space for women within a particular context. But taken on its own, it suggests on the one hand that change has nothing to do with men and on the other, that women's real agenda is to benefit at the expense of men. It can create new tensions and reinforce old ones. It may result in a kind of "gender apartheid." Carried to its logical extreme, people's most intimate relationships may become battlefields.

In recent years, there has been some rethinking on how shifts in gender balance are most effectively achieved. Women have been at the forefront of this reassessment. People who are "gender-aware" today accept that it's important, but not enough, to "work with women." The stress is on gender issues as ones of relationship, not of confrontation. The Uganda experience described in the previous chapter demonstrates this. Negotiations leading to change in the balance of power must involve both women and men, and must be satisfactory to both, so that whole groups and whole communities may go forward together, in response to a shared need.

The status quo has immense weight in any group or community. It is buttressed not just by formal authority systems but also by religion, and by mindsets that are assumed to reflect the natural order of things. Gender, and the unspoken, unacknowledged assumptions that underpin it, are integral parts of any social organization. These assumptions are therefore very difficult to alter, and something new may need to happen before people are jolted into realization of the need for change.

What happened in Kagoma was AIDS. Addressing HIV transmission became an urgent community concern. In the process of Participatory Action Research, people kept coming up against evidence that traditional gender roles were providing opportunities for transmission. Change, then, became necessary for survival.

"Gender analysis" is a phrase used to describe methodologies developed to help people monitor the process of change, and—because the development process is liable to be just as blind to gender assumptions as any other—to ensure that gender issues really *are* addressed. Gender analysis is designed to cover the initial collection of data, the setting of goals and objectives, the planning of action, implementation and, finally, evaluation.

Some strategies for change are described as "gender-neutral." This means they are assumed to be addressing situations in which gender is irrelevant. The situation has no gender implications, and everyone will benefit equally. Development consultant **Anne Skjelmerud** claims that there is no such thing. Gender is so deeply embedded in social organization that it's virtually impossible to imagine a change that has no gender implications. When there is change, there are always winners and losers. A "gender-neutral" strategy will usually be one where "man" is the norm, the gender implications have not been thought through, and the outcome leaves the existing distribution of resources and responsibilities intact. GOOD (Gender Orientation on Development) is a network set up by European Protestant development agencies to monitor gender issues in their own work. Its coordinator, Fiona Thomas, suggests that "gender-blind" might therefore be a more appropriate term to apply to this kind of strategy.

A "gender-specific" plan will be one which is intended to meet the needs of one gender without disturbing the existing distribution of resources and responsibilities. This is also an unlikely scenario. Effective change requires methodologies that will genuinely address power and distribution issues, and result in "gender-redistributive" outcomes, intended to transform existing distribution in a more egalitarian direction. For gender analysis, the crucial questions to be asked at every stage are: "What about the women? Where are the women?" And maybe also: "What will happen to the men?"

But it's not easy. In June 1995, Anne Skjelmerud was invited to take part in the evaluation team for the national AIDS program in Tanzania. This consisted of ten people: two women and eight men. "But all the men you see here are very gender-aware," she was told. "They are all married men, you see." The team never did get to see the data about the proportion of women working in executive positions in the program.

Anne stresses the importance of evaluating the unintended as well as the intended outcomes for women. She recalls a road-building program in East Africa whose goal was to involve 40

percent of local women. Well they did, and the women benefited, and the road was built. What they hadn't expected was that
there would be more malnourished children in the community at
the end of the program than at the beginning. Sarah White and
Romy Tiongco, in *Doing Theology and Development,* quote a
situation in a South Indian fishing village that ended up—as
intended—with healthier children. The women, however, were
permanently exhausted because they were now farming as well
as running their homes and taking in laundry, while many of the
men, who were unemployed, continued to sit around all day
gambling and drinking.

But a warning note. Women's development is controversial, as
the UN's Cairo and Beijing conferences (on population and
development, and women, respectively) have shown. There is
growing evidence of a worldwide backlash, particularly among
religious groupings, against the participation of women. White
and Tiongco open their chapter on gender by referring to three
examples of this. First, the fundamentalist Taliban movement
sweeping through Afghanistan has insisted that women with-
draw from work outside the home, and wear the veil, and
even UN offices have felt obliged to comply. Second, the "right
to life" movement in the USA asserts that abortion is against
God's laws. On the strength of this, some right-to-lifers terrorize
women entering clinics, and have even killed doctors who
perform abortions.

Third, there is a feeling in some parts of the developing world
that gender-awareness must be some kind of western capitalist
import, disturbing "our" women, who are really quite happy, and
interfering with religious and cultural life. An African woman
responds to this. "And your nice suit? And that smart car? Are
those in your African culture, your religion, your tradition? Seems
to me, brother, the issue's not where it's coming *from,* it's
whether you *like what's coming.*"

In Britain as I write, a top woman diplomat, tipped as the next
ambassador to Paris, has been offered a lesser appointment
instead, while the job has gone to a man from a traditional diplo-
matic background. Discrimination? No, she says. Just culture. But
until it's brought out into the open and named, that's all it will
ever be: not discrimination, just culture.

In Norway, says Anne Skjelmerud, the heads of development agencies are all men. They are all very gender-aware, very politically correct. It's getting them to ask those critical questions that's the problem, she says. "O ****!" said one, on being questioned about a particular program. "I forgot to ask about the women! But of course," he added, "women are the most important thing. I know that." I have shared this story with friends from Kenya, from Britain and from Brazil. "Yes," they say. "It's exactly the same with heads of agencies here."

It's because of this that the tools of gender analysis are so important. They should never be omitted from a process designed to produce change.

# 4

## CASA CAMBALACHE

### TRANFIGURATION

The longest journey of this remarkable year was the one that took me to Argentina, to Brazil, and then on to a seminar that was to be held, not in Beijing after all, but in South India.

I left London on the Feast of the Transfiguration. It was also the fiftieth anniversary of the dropping of the bomb on Hiroshima. How do you hold the two together—faith in transfiguration on the one hand, mindless destruction on the other? I mentioned this to the physicist friend who drove me to the airport. "Yes," he said. "But what goes on in the sun is basically the same process as the one that produced the mushroom cloud. Maybe that's the reality—that everything in the world has the potential for good or evil, life or death. Holiness or horror. So do people. Faith is not about willing away death and horror, but believing that holiness and life will ultimately triumph. For things in general. But also for me . . . the thought disintegrates into sleep."

At first light, we land in Argentina. The population of Greater Buenos Aires is around twelve million—between a third and a half of the country's total population. It is a huge city and, to a European, uncannily familiar. It might be Barcelona, or Milan. Tall modern towers mix with solid nineteenth-century civic buildings, the elegant spires of slim, pale churches which could be anywhere. And then, kneeling at the feet of the high-rise stuff, collapsing shanty towns (*barrios*) that belong more readily on the Gaza strip.

The city center has great palmy squares, full of old trees and shady cafes, a long park that seems to stretch the whole length of the city, and smart shops selling computers and perfumes and

European designer clothes. Even in the suburbs there are strings of elegant little shops and restaurants. It is a city with immense natural grace, and a sense of confidence in itself and its own status.

But where, I ask, are the poor?

## A PLACE APART

In Buenos Aires I am visiting Humberto Shikiya, from the HIV/AIDS organization COVIFAC, and **Cristina Gutierrez,** the Chilean theologian and health pastor who conducted a study of poor women and HIV that is part of the WCC's program. "Come with us," they say.

Some 3400 families live in Villa 21, which is the nearest *barrio* to downtown Buenos Aires. In the cold, gray winter afternoon, it's a place apart, crouching by the main road, sprawling into the distance. It's not a place you would visit alone, partly because it's not immediately clear how you get into it. But Cristina has lived here. Stopping by a darker patch of gray, we squeeze out of Humberto's rattly old car, wave goodbye and plunge down an alleyway. We bang on a tall iron gate, the door is flung open and we crowd into the close, dark interior of Anna's house. Mercedes Sosa sings quietly on the radio; a guitar is propped in the corner. We are warmly greeted by Barbara, Anna, Eva and Norma.

"Come," they say. "Let's go out before it gets dark." So we lock up and out we go, six of us together, which is safer. We pick our way up tiny passageways with open drains, diving between broken walls and fences. We pass piles of rusty corrugated iron, remnants of car-bodies which are somebody's Useful Things. Everything here belongs to somebody, although it may look like rubbish. Everyone seems to have a dog. We keep stopping to talk to people—cheeky children, women who greet us warmly.

Many languages are spoken here. Residents may come from Paraguay or Bolivia, Uruguay, Chile or Peru. The local FM radio, broadcasting from within the *barrio,* is called *Sapucay,* which in Guaranee means "Scream." A local group has recently won a national award for a radio series about health and education, development and community solidarity. It was called *Honrar la Vida,* which means that it's not enough to live, that honoring life and making sense of it are just as important. "What a challenge," I thought, "to make sense of living here."

But these extraordinary women have *chosen* to live here, amidst the violence and the drugs and the poverty and the danger, in homes so small and dark that you hardly know where to stand when there are more than three or four people in the room. Two of them have other occupations, and Eva has five children. They've all given their private lives to the Villa. "What else can we do?" they ask. "Things cannot go on like this."

We come to the edge of the Villa, to a dusty area of common ground surrounded by derelict factory buildings. This is the site of a new housing project, its redbrick beginnings warm against the gray evening and the gray earth and the gray piles of junk that, on closer examination in the fading light, rearrange themselves into a township.

We thread our way back through the narrow alleys, and at last we come to Casa Cambalache. This is an old house with one big room and a couple of smaller ones, donated by a woman who had to move but couldn't sell. Here the group is developing a center where women meet, make things, talk, read, and young children come to learn and play. Taken from an old tango of the same name, Casa Cambalache means "the house where everything is changing."

Cristina's research has involved a two-year program of direct accompaniment to four individual women and one of their husbands, all with HIV or AIDS, all living in Villa 21, or in another *barrio* called Ciudad Occulta (the Hidden City). Three of the women have children, and three of those children are HIV+. Another child became negative in March 1993. The program also included accompaniment of the *barrio*'s social organizations, specifically the neighborhood councils, leaders and churches.

World Bank estimates for the whole of Latin America indicate that, by the end of 1995, between 1.2 and 2 million people were infected with HIV, with more than 300,000 new infections each year. Epidemiological data suggest that the most vulnerable are girls and women between 15 and 25. This group, says the World Bank, "tends to be highly mobile or involved in tourism or commercial sex industries, but is typically the least accessible to government or international HIV/AIDS programs."

Running at 6.6 percent of all infections, Argentina has the highest proportion of these younger HIV+ women in Latin America. While intravenous drug injection has played the biggest part in the recent upsurge of numbers generally, heterosexual transmission has risen from 6 percent of the total number of cases in 1988 to 20 percent in 1994. In the same period, the number of homosexual/bisexual transmissions dropped from 67.7 percent to 27 percent (Ministry of Health & Social Action, 1995). In Argentina as a whole, the ratio of HIV+ women to men is estimated at 1:4. In areas like Villa 21, it is much higher.

Neighborhood leaders in Villa 21 and Ciudad Occulta are aware of the seriousness of the problem. It's not enough to provide facts, they say. At the community level, an HIV policy must have three separate focuses: first, to support people with AIDS and those who care for them; second, to promote conditions in which people with HIV will be motivated to avoid transmitting the virus to others; and third, to find ways of preventing uninfected people from engaging in behavior that places them at risk.

But realizing this is one thing; doing it is something else. First, the care of infected people. Social services in the *barrios* are virtually non-existent apart from the help provided by the community itself. Going to hospital means traveling great distances, perhaps to no avail unless an appointment has been made in advance.

Cristina describes the effect of HIV infection on a household. It is nearly always women who take responsibility in such a situation, and in all cases studied in Villa 21, the task of maintaining the family and caring for the sick person was performed by a woman. The main problem for such families is poverty. But where the woman herself is the infected one, the situation becomes desperate. Three of the four women the group accompanied were abandoned by their partners. Two were thrown out of their homes, one by her mother and the other by her father-in-law. This implies a housing problem that affects women particularly acutely. After periods in hospital, there is no place to come back to. One woman had her son taken away by her employers and died without ever seeing the child again. Social services are so bureaucratic and inaccessible that women with the virus often give up and live the disease "on their own," taking care of each other. At the end of the day, poverty and bureaucracy are a stronger reality than HIV infection.

This study indicates that people with HIV/AIDS take little part in policy making. Internationally, there is increasing recognition that this can't go on. As Stefano Bertozzi of WHO's Global AIDS Program put it, "If we do not understand what the most important aspects of the impact are from the perspective of the infected person, how ... can we pretend to be optimizing ... resources to minimize the impact?"

There is 60 percent unemployment in Villa 21, about average for a poor urban area, and poverty is a prime factor in causing HIV+ individuals to behave in ways that put others at risk. The world over, and throughout history, if women have no other way of feeding themselves and their families, they turn to prostitution.

In Villa 21 and Ciudad Occulta, HIV transmission is heavily bound up with the trade in illegal drugs. That's where the big money is. So sex is sold to support dependence, and to finance deals. Infected needles may be used and re-used; men who have nothing else to live for inject drugs, and then come home infected and pass the virus on. There is, really, no hope of containing AIDS without tackling the deep-seated problems of such a community. And yet, in some strange way, the virus is almost irrelevant. So you get sick with AIDS; but you may well have died of all sorts of other things long before that happens. Tomorrow is the real problem, not ten years' time. How, here, to *honrar la vida?*

During the "dirty war" from 1976-83, under the military junta, thousands of people were murdered and tens of thousands "disappeared." Governments tried to get rid of the problems of the villas by bulldozing them. Often they succeeded. In Villa 21, Eva and Norma and other women just lay down in front of the bulldozers, over and over again, until the demolition squads gave up.

Now we sit round the table together in Casa Cambalache, drinking a thick green herbal tea called *mate,* which you suck through a tube before passing it on to the next person. Nobody believes any longer in government action, say the women. It's not just our corrupt government: it's the whole global context in which it operates. With market forces and the "new economic order," it's a waste of energy campaigning for major structural change. There is a loss of faith in the possibility of any kind of genuine commitment to eliminate poverty. The only way forward, when there is no hope and so little trust, is to stake out your own space, and learn to trust each other and to build together. The basic political unit is the community itself. In the case of resisting HIV, this means the community of women and men committed to alternatives to poverty and the street culture, and committed to providing a life-project for children and young people growing up with no hope of ever being part of the dream world that holds sway "out there" beyond the borders of the *barrio.*

We pass round the *mate,* and we smoke and chat, as the bitter evening closes in and the lights come on behind the gray windows. Two of the women have meetings tonight. Tomorrow there is a party. We wander back to Anna's, and the smoky alley-ways seem suddenly safe and intimate. The electricity is on tonight. The little stores are lit up in the winter night, music drifts from the battered shacks that are somebody's home, some kids play with an old corn husk and a tin can. It's not true that it's safe, of course, or not in the way it used to be. But we choose to live here, say the women, and we are all right, so far. "I have made here," says Barbara, "the best friends that I have had in the whole of my life."

As I leave, Anna hands me a paper bag with a leather *mate*-maker and some *mate.* It's what we drink, she says, when we meet. It's in front of me now, as I write, and I'm back in the cold-warm shabbiness of Casa Cambalache—the house where you learn to believe that everything can change. "Salud, sister," I murmur, and my eyes are suddenly full of tears. For faith, for courage. For friendship and generosity shown to the stranger from another world, who has alighted fleetingly among them and now is ready to go.

## No Me Va a Pasar*

**Nidia Fonseca** comes from Costa Rica. She is an ordained minister and sociologist, working with CLAI, the Latin American Council of Churches, as secretary to the Division of Family, Women and Children. At the Vellore seminar, Nidia described the difficulties CLAI has experienced in dealing with HIV.

Having first addressed AIDS in 1989, it took three years for the churches to be convinced that more was demanded of them than

---

*It won't happen to me.

merely pastoral help for people living with the virus. The work itself raised issues of sin and sexuality that needed exploring before people could decide what the challenge was. A number of churches tried to do this, but found such a direct approach extremely difficult. So they made up their minds to look at AIDS from the broader perspective of relationships between men and women, and a joint CLAI/WCC meeting was held to talk about women and AIDS. But participants found it very difficult to talk about women and *health,* let alone women and AIDS.

A family section was then set up in CLAI. Women's groups from member churches were encouraged to talk about HIV/AIDS and its implications, and to share their thoughts with their own churches. But women found it such agony to speak out on sexual matters that this was abandoned, and an in-depth study was set up in six countries: Argentina, Costa Rica, Ecuador, Guatemala, El Salvador and Venezuela.

Nidia describes the whole process as incredibly painful. Many wounds needed healing before issues of sexual orientation, sexually transmitted diseases, domestic violence, rape and marital infidelity could be addressed within the churches, and nobody really knew how to do that. As a result of the lack of information and open discussion, much of what people believed about AIDS was nonsense: that it only attacks gay men; that Christians are protected by the Holy Spirit, etc., etc.

There was also belief that HIV/AIDS must be a disease of commercial sex workers and homosexuals. It was therefore not a legitimate concern for the churches themselves, confined as it was to "other people" outside. This state of denial made it very difficult to know where to begin. If sexuality is taboo within the church, how can you discuss transmission? How can you understand homosexuality if it's an unmentionable subject? Ask what happens if a well-behaved married woman is found to be infected with HIV and you run into a blank wall of resistance. Such a situation, it seems, is unimaginable.

The CLAI program, says Nidia, has been a fascinating exercise in analyzing human behavior in a patriarchal society. God is male. Sexuality is mediated through a culture which dictates that men should be expert in sexual intercourse but women should know nothing about it. Young men are brought up to think of women as the objects of male desire, the means for the release of sexual impulses. Love will come later, and will be associated with marriage. Thus the formative sexual encounters of youth become the "laboratory where men have sexual experience unmediated by affection," with all that implies for the quality of their future relationships with women.

If women are to be equal partners in limiting the transmission of HIV, it is essential for men as well as women to fight for a society of equal responsibilities and rights. But obvious as this may seem, says Nidia, it's not going to be easy. Women as well as men continue to believe in romantic love, where sexuality is defined by self-giving without conditions; where encouragement to use condoms is undermined by the male belief that one's manhood is proved if a woman becomes pregnant.

"What can we do to prevent AIDS?" the women in the groups asked themselves. "But we can do *nothing*," came the answer. "If our souls and bodies, our homes and our sexuality don't belong to us, how can we possibly take responsibility for preventing the disease?"

Listening to her speaking about this program, we can sense Nidia's frustration with the whole process. **Mary Engwau** from Uganda has been listening attentively. "Your presentation is coming out of anger," she comments gently. "Until you get on top of that, you will get nowhere." Working, as Nidia does, for a council of churches, I'm not so sure. Working ecumenically can be extraordinarily frustrating. Anger is exhausting, but creatively used, it may be an essential component in the energy that produces change.

## MUCHAS CHICAS*

A clatter of feet, a shout of glee. A tiny head with dark plaits peers triumphantly out of a brightly painted doorway. Three small ruffians struggle for space on the steps leading up to it, and a gaggle of little girls shriek encouragement to the one who has taken possession of the play house. The walls are covered with children's paintings, and in the surrounding rooms small heads are bent busily over their work.

Arriving at the headquarters of COVIFAC (Family and Community Life Guidance Centre), and having been told that this is

*Lots of girls.

the Protestant church's flagship AIDS/HIV program in Buenos Aires, you could be forgiven for thinking you've come to the wrong place.

Not so. This is the premises of the Parroquia Evangélica Emanuel, an ecumenical congregation born out of the union of Methodists and Disciples of Christ. Thirty years ago, it was just a church that—like many churches the world over—ran a small crèche for pre-school children on its premises. But the sixties and seventies were times of social and political chaos in Argentina. Schooling was inadequate, the streets dangerous, and social services in a state of collapse. So the congregation decided to extend the nursery to become a kindergarten, and then a primary school for local children.

Magdalena Gimena, a social worker and the wife of pastor Luis Parilla, talks of the early days, when it became clear that it wasn't just the children who were suffering but whole families. Young mothers, in particular, were in urgent need of health educa- tion and a safe place to meet and talk. Then in the seventies, as part of the price of Roman Catholic support for the Peronista regime, the government banned the use of "artificial" contra- ception. As a result, fifty family planning centers closed, one of which was COVIFAC. The premises of the (privately run) Argentina Association of Family Planning were bombed, and birth control became virtually inaccessible for Argentina's women. Abortions—all illegal—shot up and abortion-related deaths with them.

Responding to the urgent need of the women it served, COVIFAC decided to invite a family planning consultant to help them. Women who were not connected with the school or church started to attend the women's groups, and birth control advice was added to the parish's work among local people. Upstairs, above the school and the church, they now have a mini- clinic with consulting rooms where examinations can take place and intra-uterine contraceptive devices (IUDs) may be fitted.

Perhaps it was inevitable, then, that COVIFAC should be among the first organizations to take the advent of HIV seriously. On Fridays, the center is open to a group of men and women living with AIDS, along with their parents, partners and friends. At a time when the government was still denying that there was a problem, COVIFAC led the way in exploring issues of prevention, information and awareness. It publishes leaflets and runs courses and conferences. COVIFAC also has a library focused on HIV/AIDS, open daily to the public, but providing a particularly valuable service to students and teachers.

Magdalena likens the government's denial to denial of the "disappearances": 30,000 people "disappeared" during the late seventies and early eighties, and people were still saying "it won't happen to one of us." The young people of today won't let it happen, though. Bishops called for good Catholics to boycott a recent youth conference on AIDS education, in Rosario. Ten thousand young people came.

But COVIFAC's particular concern at the moment is for poor women, and their special vulnerability to HIV infection. Middle-class women tend to go out to work, and that gives them economic power and encourages them to plan their families. But poor men tend to have strong *machismo* that is satisfied by *muchas chicas*. This makes poor women particularly vulnerable. Ciudad Occulta is the "hidden city" where COVIFAC supports a youth and community center, and also a women's organization—Madres por Amor al Niño (Mother for the Love of Children).

We visit and are met by Matte. He is a former street child, 40-something, rescued by this community from the street—or at least from the drugs and drink that go with it. He has a strong sense of having been reclaimed from the refuse heap and needing to pay it back. He works for the tourism department of the social action ministry, but has a year's leave to set up development programs in Ciudad Occulta. He lives outside the *barrio* now, though, and has his own family.

Matte wants to provide alternatives to prostitution, drugs and violence. So the center has facilities for babies and children, football for teenage boys, training in skills such as plumbing and computing. Matte has friends in the government; he is respected by all the different political groups you need to please if your NGO is to succeed.

It's vital to develop networks and alliances. In November 1995, COVIFAC went into partnership with CHA (the Argentine Homosexual Community) and FUNDESO (the Foundation on behalf of Social Prisoners) to create the CASA project for people who have lost homes and jobs as a consequence of living with HIV/AIDS.

It also works with local authorities, with teachers and students, on issues of sexuality and AIDS. There *are* people in government and medical and education and church circles who realize the importance of public education and prevention. It's essential to support them and help them think strategically. People who work for change in government are more vulnerable, and in more urgent need of support, than we are.

Back in Buenos Aires, it strikes me once again that there are no poor people here. But at least now I know the truth: they're here all right, but they're locked away in the *barrios*. Then I recall Magdalena's words: "This illness is among us. It's not somewhere else."

## EVERYTHING IS RELATED TO MONEY

There are three things, I was told as a child, that one should never discuss at the dinner table. The first is money, the second politics, and the last is religion. Visiting Latin America for the first time, I was bowled over by a culture where conversations *start* with the assumption that everything is related to politics, that all politics is related to money, and that both, finally are under the judgment of God.

Hunched around the table in Casa Cambalache with the *mate* passing companionably between us and the raw gray night gathering in the battered lanes outside, the conversation slipped constantly between the local, the national and the global; between macro-economics and the cost of beans; between the God of the gospels, with that special tenderness for individual outcasts, and the God who delivered those thundering Old Testament condemnations of unjust and oppressive systems.

**Monica Arancibia** is a health promoter working with EPES (Popular Health Education) in Santiago, Chile. Chile is presented by the World Bank and other international financial institutions as a model of economic and social reform. Here, in the 1980s, financial aid packages included the order to privatize health services. These were to be supplemented by a national health fund that would manage the health services of lower-income workers. Monica speaks of the poverty of the dusty, urban *poblaciones* where she lives and works, and the devastating effects of privatization on access to, and quality of, health services.

This is not the result of ill will, says Monica. It has more to do with a completely unrealistic view of what constitutes poverty, and a system that has inflexibility and bureaucracy built into it. If, for instance, you own an iron or a refrigerator, you're not classified as poor. If you lose your job, it may take up to a year for your name to appear on the list of people eligible for free health care, so you may end up being asked to pay for prenatal care, immunization, well-baby care, and also for your children's education, even if you have no income. As a result, women are dying in childbirth again, and people stop eating so they can afford to take their children to the doctor.

Everything nowadays, it seems, is related to money and consumption. The promotion of market values is one result of a global loss of conscience about the value of human life. It's going on everywhere in the world. But the terrifying thing is that it's difficult to see what individual governments can do about it.

Current HIV prevention strategies are irrelevant to poor women in this context. WHO's macro-prevention strategies, with their emphasis on locally provided, financially affordable services, are becoming increasingly unrealistic. EPES insists that you must first concentrate on smaller-scale micro-prevention strategies that promote self-esteem, relationship skills, and a feeling that you are safe with other people.

"Which is just what Jesus did," says Monica Arancibia. She describes herself as a shanty-town woman from Chile. Politically and economically, the link between global and local, macro and micro, seems obvious to her. Listening to her in Vellore, I was revisited by a dream that haunted me in South America. If only every child growing up in a developed country could be made to spend a month sitting round a table in a Chilean (or Argentinean or Brazilian) shanty town. They would learn, there, the importance of politics, of money, and of God; and they would also learn how these are connected. And what a difference that might make to the world.

But of course it was only a dream.

# 5

# BRAZIL AND THE BODY BEAUTIFUL

## "YOU'LL NEVER UNDERSTAND BRAZIL UNLESS . . ."

The Bay of Rio de Janeiro is the most beautiful sight in the world, I've been told. It was called Rio Grande by settlers who sailed into it, believing it to be the estuary of a huge river. In Brazil, I am scheduled to attend a conference, supported by the WCC, about women, AIDS and media. How, in a week, to understand anything about a country occupying half the land-mass of South America, with a population of almost 160 million?

Unlike those earlier Europeans, though, I've done my homework, and I know that Brazil is an enormous country. It has more Roman Catholics than any other country in the world. According to World Bank figures, it is also the most unequal country in the world. The richest 20 percent has an income 27.3 times greater than the poorest 20 percent, and most economists believe that within the top 20 percent, income is highly concentrated, with a small elite enjoying one of the most sumptuous living standards in the world.

At the other end of the scale, about 98 million people have no sewers, and 30 million have no running water. An estimated 80 percent of people visiting hospital emergency rooms, and 6 percent of all admissions, are suffering from illnesses that could be prevented if the country had an adequate system of drinking water and sanitation. Since the currency changed from the *cruzeiro* to the *real* in 1994, inflation has stabilized, which has produced greater security for people who earn money. But prices, though relatively stable, are much higher, and World Bank figures indicate that the poor, who like everyone else are paying more for everything, are getting poorer.

People I meet are immensely proud of their country, and anxious to help me make the most of my time there. "You'll never understand Brazilian culture," I'm told, "unless you read the popular press / go to the beach / walk round São Paulo by night / walk round São Paulo by day / go to Carnival / visit the Northeast / take part in a religious procession / watch football / go to a motor race . . ."

"I'm here to work," I say. They look puzzled. "But you'll never understand Brazilian culture . . ."

In Rio, I stay for the first three days with **Cristina Cavalcanti,** her husband Jacov, who is a graphic designer, and three-year-old Carmen in their big, airy apartment in Cosme Velho. Cristina is a social anthropologist and writer who has analyzed the coverage of HIV/AIDS in relation to women in parts of the Brazilian press. She is also organizing the AIDS meeting. On the first morning, after breakfast, I am ready to work.

"But you must see Rio first," says Cristina. "You should not work all the time. You'll never understand Brazilian culture . . ."

I know when to quit. "OK, OK," I say. "Where do I start?"

Cosme Velho, "the old town," is full of solid old houses and apartment blocks, nineteenth-century buildings painted pink or yellow with stuccoed arches and elegant railings. It is the terminal for the little railway that groans its way up to the top of Corcovado, the jutting granite mountain from whose summit the giant statue of Christ the Redeemer towers over the city.

The train is packed with tourists, and (at 10 a.m.) throbs with the sound of partying. It pants up hill, stopping occasionally to get its breath back or to pause in a siding and let the downhill one pass. The track is through real jungle, with long snaky creepers, flame-like flowers, jack-fruits, and the occasional astounding view of sea, city, and those sharp rocky peaks that fringe the coast. We all pile out at the top and plod up the final hundred or so steps, resisting the leather sandals, parrot T-shirts, Ayrton Senna hats and the rosaries with *Cristo Redemptor* hanging from them.

And the statue really is massive. It's visible many miles out to sea—Christ the Redeemer welcoming, blessing, standing guard. They've had to build an extra viewing platform so that tourists can get far enough away to take its photo, but still it obliterates the sky. The view is extraordinary—blue blue sky, tall modern city all clustered at the foot of the mountains and along the beach. A race track. And those strange triangular mountains that push precipitately up from the sea. I feel, guiltily, that I am on holiday.

In the afternoon, I take the metro into downtown Rio with its tall modern buildings, department stores, the City Assembly building massive and proud, the elegant white palace built for the Portuguese king who made Rio the capital of Brazil. And market stalls everywhere, selling leather bags and shoes, embroidered shirts and tablecloths, bright striped waistcoats from Guatemala, brown and black woolly ones from Ecuador or Bolivia, embroidered cotton ones from Brazil.

I survive crossing the road, stand briefly with a crowd and listen to a street orator complaining about the hi-jacking of the constitution in ways that destroy local democracy, then another inveighing against new currency laws which have made the poor poorer. The street people are here too: black women with babies, crouched dully against walls; old men, drugged men, drunk men, with vacant faces and empty eyes, withdrawn and silent commentary on the noise and life, the buying and selling and passionate communication that's going on around them.

"São Paulo tomorrow," says Cristina when I get home. "You should go. You'll never understand . . ."

### "MULHER NAO E GENTE"*

São Paulo is Brazil's largest city, said to be the center of the universe or hell on earth, depending on who you're talking to. I am meeting Nancy Pereira Cardoso, an open, lovely and fearsomely intelligent woman who teaches Old Testament in the theology faculty at the Catholic University. Nancy is a Methodist pastor. She has been trying to persuade her bishop that her work among São Paulo's prostitutes should be officially recognized as a ministry, but the bishop is refusing. A pastorate, it seems, is in a *parish* with a proper *church* and a *congregation* of real *Christians*.

The "Servicio a Mulher Marginalizada" (Service for Marginalized Women) has its headquarters in little house in a cobbled cul-de-sac blessed by kittens and bougainvillaea. This is a nation-wide organization with 150 centers. Most states have an SMM center, an exception being Rio, where the bishop has banned it because he thinks it encourages prostitution. We are now at the central

*Women aren't people.

co-ordinating office that organizes training, accreditation and banking for the whole network.

From there we go for a walk, first down a busy street, past the cheap "hotels" where the women have their "programs"—dark, narrow interiors, nobody in sight within, but a lot of people hanging around chatting in the street. Picking our way round the cardboard and plastic night-shelters, we are at São Paulo's main railway station, built by a British railway company at the turn of the century. This is where you go if you want a casual, cheap pickup. The women are not really allowed inside the station, and the police beat them up if they are caught there, so they cluster on the sidewalks outside.

Dona Emilia is a big brown woman with a wide toothless smile. She is delighted to see us; there are hugs all round. I am English, *no fala portugues,* but never mind, I get a hug too. Dona Emilia is a kind of mother to the younger ones, a wise woman who has seen it all before. She is 60.

Others gather. Mara, a crack addict and alcoholic, too weird-looking and strangely behaved to get many clients, survives on passing drugs for others. She moves in a strange, convulsive way; her face is covered in the scars of old knife wounds. It is hard to tell if she is male or female. She has tried to give up the crack, but living on the streets, it's impossible. Silvia is a good-looking black woman whose family, in the northeastern interior, doesn't know she does this work but does need the money. I am haunted, today, by a verse from Psalm 27: "I believe that I shall see the goodness of the Lord in the land of the living." What does that mean for Dona Emilia and the others?

We chat, and then go. Their busy time starts at about 4:30 p.m. when men are going home from work. Especially on Friday, with the weekend coming up. God bless you, says Dona Emilia to me. A powerful blessing, says Nancy.

Immediately round the corner from the station, we are in São Paulo's "Bridal City." Every single store in the street sells wedding dresses. The windows are full of them—bouffant white satin with sleeves like pineapples; cream with long lacy trains fanned out against the wall like peacock tails; white with pink rose-buds with matching headdress and bridesmaids' dresses in pink with white rosebuds. Whole shops sell nothing but headdresses and satin shoes. Young girls wander along, window-shopping, dreaming dreams. In each glittering entrance stands a formidable woman whose task is to entice them in and make them buy. This street is the gateway to the charmed world of marriage, home, children. Pass through here, and happiness is yours. Fail to make it and who knows? You might end up on the streets with Mara and Silvia and Dona Emilia.

Later, I go for a walk in the square and note that I am being followed by a young black lad. I turn to face him and let him pass. Without pausing, he cruises past me, arm extended, and makes a grab for the camera I am clutching in my hand. Is this what happens to the children of Mara, Silvia and Dona Emilia? These women live so close to the breadline that they can't afford to set rules that would control fertility and protect them from infection. The Brazilian government is promoting birth control and conducting public education on AIDS. But the Catholic Church as an institution is still totally opposed to both.

This incident makes me cautious, though, and later, before I leave the hotel and go out on the town, I stow my money and passport in pockets so inaccessible that even I can't get at them without undressing. I remember my mantra though ("You'll never understand Brazil unless . . ."), and sally forth to find some food.

The streets are humming, shops still open, restaurants beginning to fill up. I pass clubs and cinemas advertising *sexo exotico, sexo erotico* and *sexo explicito,* and find a restaurant with pink tablecloths where I am greeted and cared for with great warmth and kindness by the owner. Major (but discreet) excavation required to get at money; then back to hotel, unscathed and restored, to bed. I go to sleep thinking I've learned quite a lot about Brazilian culture already, and wondering if I qualify, yet, to start on the work I'm here to do.

## CONDOMS ARE SEXY

Back in Rio, I'm introduced by Cristina Cavalcanti to her study of the way Brazilian media have dealt with the HIV/AIDS pandemic. As in other Latin American countries, Cristina says, the media profile of HIV/AIDS in Brazil has associated the virus with homosexual men, drug users and commercial sex workers. In the early 1990s, a new category entered the public consciousness—the monogamous housewife, clearly a victim of an unfaithful and/or bisexual man, but shifting from victim to vector status when she becomes pregnant, since she then puts at risk what the *Tribuna da Imprensa* describes as "innocent and defenseless fetuses."

Once the possibility of heterosexual transmission of HIV was confirmed, AIDS became a matter of public interest and started to appear on the programs of schools and churches. Sex and sexuality, sexual choice and orientation became matters for the media, bringing the private sphere into the public spotlight, but without either disturbing the homosexual image of the epidemic in Brazil, or increasing the level of awareness of the social conditions of women's lives. On the contrary, the suggestion that HIV in women only becomes a matter of concern when it enters the mainstream nuclear family has—if anything—reinforced the images (heterosexuality, monogamy, home-making, having sex in order to have children) that give meaning to "being a woman." "In spite of many researchers' recognition that women's subordination directly contributes to their vulnerability to HIV," says Cavalcanti, "the press fails to point out that this is a factor to be taken into account in public health policy."

Cavalcanti has analyzed the representation of sexuality, safer sex and HIV/AIDS prevention in three Brazilian women's magazines, *Claudia*, *Nova* and *Marie Claire*, each with its own target or ideal reader. I have quoted extensively from her written work in this section, and also from her presentation to the Vellore seminar.

First *Claudia*. Modeled on the North American *Good House-keeping*, *Claudia* is aimed principally at the "traditional" woman whose identity is centered on her role as wife, housewife and mother. It aims to offer the reader ways of fulfilling these tasks better. In discussing psychology and sexuality, *Claudia* commonly adopts an intimate and confessional tone. This is abandoned when it refers to AIDS. ". . . You may be thinking to yourself: 'This does not concern me.' And it doesn't. But it could be a problem for one of your friends who is newly divorced."

The lens of domesticity through which the magazine's worldview is filtered attempts to distance the problem. The virus, with the danger and deviance it represents, always comes from outside the home, as a threat to its comfort and security. While mentioning the existence of condoms, and the desirability of women persuading men to use them, it offers no convincing arguments for doing so. It offers no strategies for negotiating safer sex. There is no suggestion that different or safer sexual practices might be possible, or that readers might adopt a more open and forthright attitude to sexuality.

One of the most difficult challenges for HIV/AIDS prevention, says Cavalcanti, is how to present the subject to married women. "How can the idea of safer sex be introduced into a relationship that is, in itself, synonymous with security? How is it possible to express a lack of trust within a marriage or stable relationship without destroying the very trust on which the relationship is supposed to be based?" Apart from warnings about the risk posed by bisexual men, *Claudia* does not consider this question.

The magazine *Nova*, the Brazilian version of *Cosmopolitan,* speaks to the woman who has her own career, but for whom sex, preferably with her future husband, is the crux of her existence. Success in her career will make her sexier, and more attractive to "successful" men. For *Nova,* as for *Claudia,* the danger for women is not HIV itself, but bi-sexual men, who are unidentified, cagey and elusive, and whose "real nature," hidden within marriage, could emerge at any minute.

"It is so difficult to identify them," warns the magazine, "that most people are not sure whether they even know one."

*Nova*'s approach to safer sex is consistent with the precarious balance the magazine maintains: a defense of women's sexual assertiveness and access to sexual pleasure on the one hand, underpinned on the other by a set of values defined by dominant male cultural standards. Look at this list of possible solutions, which *Nova* offers to women concerned about the risk of HIV:

- using a vibrator to guarantee pleasure, with a partner or alone;
- faithfulness to one partner;
- abstinence;
- a relationship with a married man who is expected to be faithful both to his spouse and mistress;
- relationships with men from rural areas who have not been exposed to urban life and its evils.

Cavalcanti points out *Nova*'s combination of compliance with Catholic values (abstinence and faithfulness), with rejection of them (safer extramarital relationships), and this in the largest Catholic country in the world.

In *Nova,* unlike *Claudia,* it is the woman who is in charge of proposing, buying and putting on the condom. *Nova* talks about these new practices as an expression of women's self-esteem, wrapping them in "an aura of modernity, making them seem as ordinary as wearing lipstick." In addressing women's paranoia about bi-sexual men, it urges them to be selective, although it admits how difficult this is to achieve without invading the privacy of another person. One of the women interviewed sums it up like this:

> I won't go to bed with a man without knowing who he has been with besides me. But you need a certain amount of intimacy in order to ask questions about sex. How can you achieve that kind of intimacy with a man before you have had sex with him?

So although *Nova* manages to separate sex from reproduction, and to affirm women's right to take the initiative in sexual matters, it has not moved outside the narrow circle of genitality. The range of options offered to women, says Cavalcanti, "remains limited by an image of sexuality that ignores the actual experience of women and takes male sexuality, centered on vaginal intercourse, as its model."

When *Marie Claire* was launched in 1991, it was aiming at something different for women—to be "daring, pioneering, able to break through the taboos" and expand its attention beyond the themes traditionally considered "feminine." Its target audience is the woman who brings together the apparently irreconcilable: professional ambition and family, care for her appearance and ten hours work a day, lack of time and the desire to cook that very special supper, concern about the external world and total attention to the inner world.

Not surprisingly, *Marie Claire* speaks to a variety of different female lifestyles and images—the married, the young and ambitious, the lesbian. Health is an important theme. It stresses the necessity of taking responsibility for one's health, treating the body as something that can be transformed but needs constant supervision and maintenance. In relation to the HIV epidemic, women must be well-informed, self-reliant and firmly convinced of the value of safer sex, which they should impose on their partners where necessary. Any idea that this might prove to be difficult is met by the suggestion that all women need do is to use their "natural" feminine sensuality and grace. This is demonstrated in the magazine's "Condoms are sexy" campaign; one of its advertisements has a man describing an affair with a woman who was so skilled in condom use that he did not even notice her putting one on as she caressed his penis.

A survey of readers' reactions to the "Condoms are sexy" campaign showed that 60 percent of the women who responded did not feel inhibited about suggesting condom use to their partners, while 89 percent said condoms did not interfere with their pleasure, and 81 percent said they did not regard marriage as a haven against AIDS.

For *Marie Claire,* the business of selecting a sexual partner seems not to be a problem. The reader knows where she stands, she "looks after herself," and safer sex is a feature of a better and healthier life. By appealing to a Brazilian version of narcissism, the magazine links safer sex to personal growth and self-love, which in turn is linked to the "excessive preoccupation with the body among the middle and upper strata of the Brazilian population." Thus it becomes part of the strict discipline demanded by the "body beautiful," which includes dieting, body-building, the use of electronic instruments to mold the body, and the widespread appeal of plastic surgery. "From this perspective," says Cavalcanti, "the containment of the self which is required for AIDS prevention becomes one more restriction to comply with, an extension of other aspects of body control, like control over fertility and the re-shaping of the body in order to fulfill the new aesthetic demands."

For *Marie Claire,* the responsibility for safer sex is the woman's. But even though this reflects contemporary preoccupations with the healthy life, body control and the affirmation of women's power in sexual relations, its focus—as in *Claudia* and *Nova*—is on sexual intercourse. All three magazines present condoms as synonymous with safer sex, and rarely (if ever) consider the possibility that sexual activities other than vaginal intercourse might be equally pleasurable for women.

## WHO AM I?

*Claudia, Nova* and *Marie Claire* are successful magazines that sell, between them, almost one million copies a month. If each is read by an average of five people, that places the total readership at somewhere between four and five million, almost all of them women, and mostly within the better-off sections of Brazilian society. The magazines have carefully formulated marketing strategies, and while the answers they come up with may not satisfy all their readers, their approaches and attitudes must be assumed to appeal to substantial groups within the population, and to reflect the questions each group believes the HIV epidemic to be posing. It should be noted that they do not address the association between HIV transmission and domestic violence, or between HIV transmission and poverty; and none of them is recorded as dealing seriously with HIV education for children. Nevertheless, some important conclusions can be drawn from the study as a whole—conclusions which spotlight some of the paradoxes faced by women living and loving in a time of AIDS.

In spite of being the least radical of the magazines, *Claudia* raises some of the most difficult issues. Its view of marriage and love is not just a more romantic one. It is also more rooted in traditional values. *Claudia* therefore takes seriously the fact that when women fall in love, they may well dismiss risks, and are likely to ignore commonsense rules about safer sex. According to *Nova* and *Marie Claire*, for whom sexual assertiveness and passion are more likely focuses than love, this is a naïve view. Their readers should know better than that. And yet the *Claudia* approach asks questions that may ring bells for women in many cultures.

Condoms are valued not just because of the protection they provide. They also make it possible to avoid asking too many questions about a partner's other relationships. The past may be ignored; it will not be necessary to spoil the fervor of seduction with inconvenient questions. And yet the application of the condom itself interrupts what Cavalcanti describes as "the here and now of the sexual act."

In choosing a contraceptive method, women face a parallel dilemma. In general, women say they prefer an "invisible" method which will allow both partners to forget the fact that the encounter might have undesired consequences. The regular use of condoms against HIV infection carries a constant reminder of risk, a distressing association between sex on the one hand, and disease and death on the other.

For a variety of reasons, then, condoms may be a source of conflict. They are visible. They imply lack of trust. They interrupt an act which is supposed to be spontaneous. They are thought to make sexual relationships more impersonal. Both literally and symbolically, they constitute a barrier between lovers at what they hope will be a moment of great intimacy. Taken alongside the other main elements in AIDS prevention campaigns (the need to reduce the number of sexual partners, and to be selective in one's choice), it may be that both men and women will find the cost to the spontaneity of passion too great.

Cavalcanti draws a number of conclusions from this research. First, she suggests that there is a need to look beyond the recommendations of the women's magazines she's studied. As a first step, she says, women need to develop a language that helps them to include men in taking responsibility for sexual and reproductive health. If you're brought up not to talk about sex at all, and have never learned to do so, how are you going to negotiate safer sex, particularly with a less-than-enthusiastic partner?

Next, the risk of HIV infection challenges partners to explore ways other than vaginal intercourse of giving and receiving sexual pleasure. Women often say how much they value closeness, talking, kissing, stroking and hugging; how much they regret the speed with which sexual encounters become genital ones when men are in control. Instead of adopting male patterns of sexuality, sexual assertiveness for women might involve considering truthfully and courageously what kinds of sexual behavior they really do enjoy most, and trying to make them a priority in sexual encounters.

Cavalcanti looks forward to the development of vaginal microbicides for HIV protection, while recognizing that this will take a long time. Even then, she reflects, upper- and middle-class women will be the ones to benefit, as is the case with other provisions for sexual and reproductive health such as fertility control and safe abortions.

At the end of the day, she says, although media and public education campaigns are important, the support of community networks is the really crucial factor in behavior change. The ability to practice safer sex seems primarily to relate to a sense of belonging to an identity group or community which perceives for itself that this is a matter of importance. European studies of bi-sexual and homosexual men show that adoption of safer sex strategies depends on "information, proximity to people with HIV, and personal vulnerability." But what helps make safer sex habitual are the social relations and shared culture within a

particular identity group—in this case the gay community itself—
which enhance self-esteem and community identification, so that
behavior change becomes both possible and desirable to individuals within the group.

The women's magazines studied are an identity group of a kind
in that they create a sense of communication between women,
affirm a particular moral, cultural or philosophical position, and
provide an informal exchange network. This is not enough,
though, says Cavalcanti. The culture that determines behavior is
too strong. Effective change can only really come from the context of women's everyday realities, and with the support of an
effective flesh and blood community, recognizing a common
agenda, communicating in a common language, and moving forward together to provide an alternative to the prevailing culture.

## O Que É Novo?*

It's carnival time. A multicolored crowd comes tumbling down
the street—clowns and animals and men on stilts, children
screaming with delight, riding on their parents' shoulders. The
music plays. Watching the procession from an upstairs window is
a beautiful girl. "Use camisinha!" (Use a condom!) she is calling.
In the densest part of the crowd, we notice that a tall red
condom has appeared, dancing along the street and throwing
hearts to the delighted people.

In Brazil, public education campaigns on television, like this
one, are often colorful and entertaining. A WCC meeting brings
twenty-five women and five men from NGOs and government
together with journalists from newspapers, magazines and radio
to take a wider-ranging look at media responses to HIV. Why, ask
the NGOs, don't you portray HIV/AIDS in a more responsible
way? Why can't you see, respond the media people, that we have
to sell papers or die? What we publish must be news.

What, then, is News? Laura Capriglione of the high-circulation
*Veja* tries to answer. HIV first became Real News in Brazil when
the singer Cazuza died of it in 1990. In the beginning, it was
reported among the rich and famous, and they are always News.
Today, it is more likely to affect the poor and the drug-addicted,
who are not News. The one News thing in recent years has been

*What's news?

the infection of women. But it is very difficult to report on this. *Veja* depends on individual testimonies and interviews that personalize an issue and make it interesting to the readers, but they can never find women who are willing to talk publicly about the disease, and about the real feelings and conflicts it produces. AIDS issues, Laura says, need people with the guts to talk about their lives, about how they deal with husbands and children, about death.

The NGO response is sharp. First, in personalizing the issue, newspapers and magazines make sure that nobody tackles the political and economic implications, such as funding priorities, poverty and government policy. Second, it is irresponsible of the press to put selling papers before public education.

But the press is not there to educate, it's there to inform, say the journalists. In many parts of the world, say the NGOs, the *main* task of the press is public education.

The focus shifts. Selling papers, like selling cars, often relies on images of women as objects of sexual desire. This, it is said, promotes a view of women as instruments of male pleasure. The journalistic vision of women is based on the romanticized vision of a woman "giving herself" to a man. But this is the reality, says Monica Serino, editor of *Marie Claire.* The fact that we acknowledge that women feel like this doesn't mean we are not addressing their problems; it means we are facing the truth. The biggest risk group of all are the women in love.

But how do we change that? someone asks. Brazilian culture is obsessed with romanticism and eroticism. Sickness and death are unmentionable, because they don't fit in with the prevailing culture of eroticism. In a time of AIDS, this is fantasy-land and the media should know better than to encourage it.

An energetic young woman from Recife speaks. She runs a local radio program for women in rural areas in the Northeast. "None of this," she says thoughtfully, "has any relevance at all to the job I do. You are talking to high-class women who read newspapers and can make choices about their lives. But Brazil is two worlds. For poor women from the interior, the culture of the middle-class press is foreign. Radio is an ideal medium, provided it addresses the realities of their lives."

Instead of generalizing, says Cristina Cavalcanti, let's try a "current reading" approach to the issue, as it appears in particular contexts and disciplines. For epidemiologists, for instance,

AIDS is unlikely to maintain the priority it's enjoyed in recent years. The epidemiology of AIDS is having to be reconstructed as the epidemic profile changes.

Are we really saying that AIDS has stopped being a crisis and become routine? asks a woman's magazine journalist. Now that *is* News!

It's clearly very complicated. But for me, three things do emerge. First, that the reality of women's lives is the starting point for education, and you cannot generalize about that; second, that local radio is an exceptionally powerful medium for doing this; and third, that the main tools needed for this dialogue are accurate monitoring of media coverage, and convincing research into its effects. Since this meeting, Cristina Cavalcanti has embarked on research, sponsored by the World Association for Christian Communication and based at ISER, on women's readings of sexuality and gender relations in the media.

## THE BODY BEAUTIFUL

I leave this fascinating meeting with Chris Horak, an anthropologist from the University of Illinois, whose husband is Brazilian. We sit by a pool in a rooftop bar drinking beer. It's high enough to be cool. We're surrounded by night-lit Rio: the hilltop favelas, the beaches, the Sugarloaf mountain and, on the skyline, *Cristo Redemptor,* floodlit.

"You won't understand anything about Brazilian culture," says Chris, "until you've been to the beach." So I catch the bus, next morning, past Copacabana ("too crowded") to Ipanema Beach. Arrive at 9:30 a.m. and, oh yes! mile upon mile of white sand visible through the palm trees, a great granite peak at the end of the beach, and in the angle of peak and beach, a town. Great swelling walls of water explode into white foam and bear down upon the beach. Already there are surfers, slicing towards the beach, then going back and mounting the next towering breaker, twisting and turning and subsiding into the shallows.

Why didn't I bring my swimsuit? Mind you, the *Lonely Planet Guide* says there's no point in taking a swimsuit with you to Brazil because however skimpy you think it is, you'll find there's too much cloth between the seams. Well, they're right. Around me, near-naked people of all ages are doing press-ups and aerobics. In Brazil, the body is definitely on show—any size, any age, as long as it's brown.

I sit for a while, watching the various groupings—an energetic, sand-spraying men's world of ball games, press-ups, surfing, committed sunbathing; an adult women's world of black maids and white children, mothers and families. There are chattering flocks of nubile nymphets in dental floss bikinis; and a few middle-aged women strolling companionably down the hard sand. The different worlds don't appear to meet, although the nymphets spend a disproportionate amount of time contemplating the ball games. Fathers playing with children are conspicuously absent. The only black people are the maids.

It's the Brazilian winter now. Coming from a chilly northern country, where flesh is firmly under wraps for most of the year, it's hard to imagine what it must be like to live in a country where you can take your clothes off in public with pride for virtually the whole year round. Here I really do get the feeling of what Brazilian eroticism is about, the eroticism which Brazilians themselves blame for the *machismo,* the uninhibited sexuality which drives the progress of HIV, the commitment to the body and the accompanying confidence that it is beautiful.

But if the beach is a demonstration of what "Brazilian culture" is all about, then the beach says this as well: that to be a Real Man means being strong and tanned, sexy and competitive; to be a Real Woman means living in a world of women and children; to be poor is to be invisible; and to be black means that you don't come into the picture at all except for the services you are able to offer.

Are these, then, the dominant myths of Brazilian culture, the assumptions to which any pressure for changed behavior must speak? If they are, and we are right in assuming that the subordination of women is the entry point for HIV, then it is not just within individual social groups in Brazil that one must look for the windows of transmission: it's in the great chasms that divide groups and people within society as a whole; it's within the mismatch between, on the one hand, the myths that underpin people's vision of their own culture, fed as they are by media, and on the other hand, the real but conflicting experience of huge sections of it.

In this respect, Brazil, although quite unlike it in so many ways, is no different from my own society or, probably, from yours.

# 6

## INDIAN SUMMER

### Not Beijing

In South India, it is monsoon time. The flight from Singapore bucks and reels through the mother and father of a thunderstorm. In Madras, there is a power cut as well—pitch black night, walls of water, the blessed earth beneath our feet.

It should, of course, have been Chinese earth. This seminar was originally planned as part the World Council of Churches' participation in the UN Women's Conference in Beijing. If this were to prove impossible, where would we hold it? **Sara Bhatta-charji,** who is a professor of community health at the Christian Medical College, Vellore, was going to be part of the group in any case. When **Jacob John** offered to arrange for us to hold it there, it seemed like a gift from God.

This seminar was crucial to the whole "Women and Health and the Challenge of HIV/AIDS" program. Thirty people took part, many of whom have appeared in the earlier chapters of this book. All of the work supported by the WCC and described earlier was presented at the seminar. Its objective was to consider this in the light of the experience of those present, to reflect on it theologically, and to see what kind of action to recommend to the churches. So this book could equally well have been an account of a meeting.

But the problem with meeting reports is that they are never as fascinating as the meetings themselves, and tend to end up, quite quickly, in the backs of filing cabinets. We therefore made the decision to report on the program in a different way. Although the people responsible for the African and Latin American programs were there, neither their presentations nor the discussions they provoked appear here; they have been included instead in the chapters relating to those regions. Margareta Sköld's presentation on women's health and Anne Skjelmerud's on gender analysis both appear in the position and form in which they should be most helpful to the reader. And yet nothing in this book would have been possible without the process of reflection and distillation that took place among the thirty remarkable people who gathered in Vellore, South India, from five continents, in the last days of August, 1995.

## "INTO A BROAD PLACE . . ." (*Ps. 18:19*)

Madras to Vellore is a slow and bumpy drive of some 130 kilometers. It's still dark when we leave Madras: dark, and still raining, the tangled traffic heavy in the sodden streets. But it clears as we leave the city behind. The rain stops. The slow morning wakes. Women amble along with water pots on their heads. An early bullock cart. A lean man in a *lunghi* relieves himself into a ditch. A naked child stands dazed outside his palmleaf house, rubbing his eyes. Over the paddy, a blanket of mist. A thread of pink, a broader glow, and by 8:30 a.m. we are driving westward, our backs warmed by the red blaze of the Indian dawn.

The fields unfold—scrub and dust, deserted half-finished concrete buildings. The startling green of the paddy fields. The teaming roadside life that is India, of people and animals and bullock carts, of wandering cows and kamikaze bikes and murderous trucks. Now the ancient jagged hills of North Arcot district emerge from the haze. The villages get larger and busier, we cross the Palar bridge, and we are coming into Vellore.

Here the traffic thickens, but our driver is now on home ground. He settles his hand on the horn, his foot on the accelerator, and goes. The tall cream walls of the hospital flash by, then the market; Vellore's famous old fort and temple, and the green *maidan,* where the troops used to exercise. The circus is in town. A blare of music, an approaching crowd, our driver jams on the brakes and we stop. Today is a religious holiday, when Ganesh, the plump, friendly, elephant god, is borne on shoulders through the town. Ganesh himself is improbably naked-looking and defenseless, and yet a popular and approachable god, a remover of obstacles, a promoter of prosperity, his best friend the despised rat who sits at his feet. It's to Ganesh that you pray for the success of a new venture.

The procession passes. We can move again. And now we are in another world—the tree-shaded, orderly world of the medical college campus, where the community health training block is sited. And here, three days later, on Sunday afternoon, I am able at last to sit and gather my thoughts.

It would be difficult to find a more fitting place than the Christian Medical College, Vellore to hold a meeting on women and AIDS. A hundred years ago, Indian cultures would not allow women to be seen by male doctors. As a result, childbirth was a dangerous business, and many women died unnecessarily. CMC Vellore was set up by the American doctor Ida Scudder with the object of training women as midwives and doctors, so that they could meet the desperate health care needs of Indian women.

CMC Vellore is an important institution in the history of the world church's struggle to make a reality of a Christian vision of health care. Its story is told in my previous book, *Whose Ministry?* The months I spent here, writing this (and also *There Rest Thy Feet,* a little book about its community health work, published in 1989) have been among the formative experiences of my life. It was here that I met my husband; here that I made some of my best friends. I am overwhelmed by how lovely it is to be back with a new job to do, and also by the extraordinary set of chance events that have made it possible.

I am also impressed by the wonderful new community health training block, where most of us are staying, and where our seminar is to be held. A shaded courtyard. A white-painted flagged lobby with cane chairs and flowers on the low cane table. It's quiet here, and there's enough of a through-breeze for us not to need the fans. Somewhere, the choir is practicing for this evening's service in the college chapel. There are snatches of music, the odd burst of laughter. From the kitchen comes the clatter of dishes being washed; from the surrounding treetops, laced against the sky, an arch of birdsong with its flat, resentful bass-line of barking crows.

Crouched over *The Hindu* newspaper is **Caroline Kruckow** from the German development agency EZE, which has provided the funding for the change of venue to Vellore. *The Hindu* has a report of yesterday's opening ceremony in Beijing, a two-page feature on the Indian delegation, and a number of horror stories about conditions generally, the weather in particular. Cristina Cavalcanti, with whom I stayed in Rio, is reading an Indian women's magazine and smoking. Everybody else is asleep, or else reading in their rooms.

This morning we've been to different local churches, but tonight we'll worship together, with staff and students, in the round, airy college chapel. "The Lord brought me out into a broad place," says the psalmist in this morning's reading from my little book of Bible texts. We have come from the corners of the earth with our different experiences, our different cultures, our different stories. And to try, somehow, to work out together just why it is that women's health and HIV/AIDS constitute such important challenges to the churches.

## A SHAKING HAND

It's appropriate that we should be doing this in India. The center of gravity of the AIDS epidemic is shifting from Africa to Asia, and barring an unexpected breakthrough in medical research, WHO estimates that by the year 2000, the majority of new cases will occur in Asia. In some cases, the rate of increase in HIV prevalence outstrips anything Africa has yet known. Its two primary focuses are currently (a) India and (b) Cambodia, Thailand and Myanmar.

HIV has become established across Asia in places where high-risk behavior relates to intravenous drug use, and where commercial sex is common. But the sex trade is no longer just a matter of poor women making a bit of extra income. It is a matter of great concern that—in Thailand and the Philippines at least—the trade in women and children has, in recent years, become an international multi-million-dollar industry, driven from Europe, Japan and North America.

Asian countries, however, have had greater difficulty than others in acknowledging that there is a problem. Officially, India now recognizes the urgency of the challenge. The money that has come from the World Bank for AIDS, says Sara Bhattacharji, is the same as a whole year's health budget. But apart from blood bank control, it's ineffective in getting through to the villages. At heart, she says, the government is still in a state of denial.

When it comes to recognizing officially that a major health challenge is connected with sex, denial comes easily in a country where sex is officially taboo. In India generally, open demonstrations of physical affection are unacceptable. Men and women, traditionally, do not dance together. Sexual matters are not discussed, and homosexuality is mentioned only as "a western problem." And yet there are millions of commercial sex workers, boys as well as women.

This denial of sexuality affects everyone, of course. But it particularly affects women, who are traditionally modest about mentioning sexual or gynecological matters. Sara describes a woman of 50 who suffered from vaginal bleeding for two years before she came to the hospital. When she did come, she found herself unable to tell the doctor why, and went away with pills for headaches. After several visits, she did manage eventually to explain, but by then she was in the terminal stages of uterine cancer.

In a study of two villages in Maharashtra state, an astonishing 92 percent of women were found to have gynecological or sexually transmitted diseases, with an average of 3.6 diseases each (*Bang et al., 1989*). Infections made up 50 percent of this burden of suffering. But only 8 percent of the women had ever had a gynecological examination, although 55 percent said they were aware that there was a problem. If nothing else, this suggests a potentially lethal combination of sexual mobility on the one hand, and cultural inability to face its consequences on the other.

This sense of unreality is reinforced by male myths. Jacob John quotes a confidential survey among male college teachers. Most believed that masturbation was more harmful than having sex with a prostitute. In this group, the average length of an (unerect) penis was declared to be 12 inches; the average length of intercourse was one hour.

**Jaruwan Wutti** has similar stories coming from Thailand. She describes a conference for Thai Christian leaders held in 1992. Here, the attitude was, firstly, "It serves them right"; secondly, "AIDS is a medical problem"; and, thirdly, "if the doctors are afraid of HIV, we should be even more afraid."

Kimachandra Sind, general secretary of the Church of Christ in Thailand, describes AIDS as "a prophet in the wilderness" to the Thai churches. Setting up a project in Chiang Mai, where the epidemic is worst, CCT concentrated on a model of community-based care that stressed the importance of team members making personal relationships with people with AIDS and those who cared for them. This was OK. It was when they started to campaign for more effective sex education among young people that church people started to complain. "It's impossible to talk about sex in a Christian way," people said.

More money has been spent on HIV seminars in Chiang Mai than anywhere else in the world, says Jaruwan. But the situation hasn't changed. And religious people don't help. The Christians and Muslims say it's God's punishment; the Buddhists that it's "karma." This experience, says Jaruwan, has been a moment of truth for the Thai government, which for the first time has admitted that it is not omnipotent. In acknowledging the effectiveness of NGOs in dealing with HIV, it has taken its first halting steps towards a different model of working with communities.

We are joined for the Asia consultations by Dr. J. P. Muliyil, an epidemiologist with CHAD, the Community Health and Development program of CMC Vellore. In the early nineties, CHAD did a leprosy study in a small area of Vellore Town which had many commercial sex workers. In parallel to this, they set up a limited community health program, offering condoms, etc., and found that in learning about the area, they were making friends with the women. What were their working conditions? Why were they there?

Shanti's story is a common one. She left home at 16 after a row with her parents over a boyfriend. He stayed with her for a week and then left. She was penniless. But then, just when she was really desperate, she met a nice man who offered her lodging and a job. But first, he said, she needed a Rs2000-3000 down payment. "I'll fix it for you," said the "agent," and took her to a moneylender, who then sold his interest on to an "owner." The interest on this loan was said to be 10 percent. 10 percent *a day*, which works out to 230 percent interest a year.

Shanti started to take paying customers from among the young men and construction workers locally. She could take five to ten customers a day, or more at the weekend. Most of them did not wear condoms. At first she didn't know it was important, and when she did, she could afford neither the condoms nor the luxury of turning down a man who refused to use one. Out of what she earned, she had to give one-third to her "owner," plus what was needed to pay off the debt. Having left home to find freedom, she found herself trapped in a cycle of debt and exploitation from which there was no escape.

J. P. describes the experience of working in this area. "We set out wanting to change the people," he said, "but the end result was that we ourselves started to change. We found ourselves standing round in the street laughing, with little groups of sex workers." At first he was afraid of being seen by people who might know him. But then, he reflected, "Those are not the thoughts of a Christian. They're the thoughts of a Pharisee."

The area had become the focus of an HIV micro-epidemic. One survey of young men between 18 and 23 showed that twelve out of fifteen were HIV-positive. If a new girl came, she would very soon become infected, without any way of protecting herself. J. P. found it all deeply disturbing. He was overwhelmed by the women's vulnerability, and by the feeling that he just could not allow these men to go on having unprotected sex. But what could he do? The oppression of women, which was endemic, had become the entry point for the virus in this community. If the women were powerless to prevent themselves from becoming infected, then medical practice, as he'd been brought up to understand it, was useless.

And his religion was no help. Advise condoms, says the church, and you sanction immorality. "Where," thought J. P., "is the greater immorality? . . . Suppose when I meet God, I were to say 'Lord, Lord, I was a good man. I didn't smoke, I didn't drink.' Would the Lord then say to me, 'Yes my son, and you became so good that you couldn't communicate with the ones I love.' Because Jesus," says J. P., "had a special affection for these people— the disabled, the ones with leprosy, the sex workers. If we alienate ourselves from these, then we alienate ourselves from God. And yet," he says, "I have so little to give. All I can offer is a shaking hand."

"What," I ask, half-joking, "is an epidemiologist doing getting so worked up about real people? I thought," I say, "that you were meant to concentrate on figures and statistics and transmission rates."

"I can't do it like that any more," says J. P. "How can I understand a figure or a statistic unless I've held the hand it represents?

The people we're talking about are the same as us," he says. "By the way we treat them, we know just how much like Jesus we've become."

And that, more than anything, is the lesson he's learned from the work he's been describing. "I told you!" says Jacob John. "I told you he's the world's best epidemiologist!"

## "WE ARE LEARNING!"

The soul of India is in the villages, said Gandhi. It's time now to leave the leafy comfort of the training center and go on a visit to the women of SHARE, the trading society which was set up by economically active local women when governmental control over their co-operatives was stepped up. Rani, SHARE's secretary, applied to attend the Beijing meeting but was turned down. "A woman is somebody who is looked down on in society," she says. "We felt we had to have a place where we could do something for women."

The society buys handicrafts from local co-operatives, then markets them, mainly to foreign organizations. They have been very successful, and are keen to spread the word, not just about the business venture, but about the new perspectives the work has given them on life generally. They are trying to encourage women to bring into the open the subjects that are so difficult to talk about. They themselves, for instance, are now confident enough to say "no" to female infanticide, and some members recently traveled to Kolyanbatam, near Madurai, to talk to a similar but newer group of women about this experience.

Now here we are, on this shimmering afternoon, sitting in the shady work room of the SHARE center. There are some twenty Indian village women, graceful in their colored saris, sitting, most of them, on mats on the floor. Baskets and mats and bags and scarves and broad, shady hats are stacked on the shelves. And then our own party, nineteen of us, African, Thai, European, Caribbean, Latin American, mainly (but not all) women, gathered from the corners of the earth on the day when the Beijing conference opens, a kind of mini-NGO Forum in our own right.

First, their own lives, and the obstacles to equality they face. They tell of girls and boys brought up differently, cultural differences in terms of education and marriage. And not just the fact that men don't allow women to progress, but that women are brought up to lack confidence in their ability to do so. "It's because we don't want to go on in that way that we come here," says Kasturbi.

From the Africans come questions about divorce, and about the inheritance of property. But divorce is not acceptable for women in India. In what circumstances might it be acceptable? Violence? Alcoholism? Illicit relationships? It happens, say the women, but it is never acceptable. You would be ostracized. You just have to put up with it. As regards property, there are laws, but it is sometimes difficult. A woman has more freedom in society if she stays with her husband.

"How important is sex?" asks Cristina Cavalcanti, with Brazilian openness. There is a flutter and a ripple of discussion. Then oneof the Indian women answers, in Tamil. "They say they don't understand the question," says Sara, who is interpreting. Cristina rephrases it; the same response comes back. "Supposing," asks Mary Engwau from Uganda, "supposing the man becomes impotent? Suppose he has another woman? Suppose he has AIDS? What then?" It's not a reason for separation. . . . Marriage is about more things than just sex. . . . It's marriage that's important, comes the answer. "Well," says Christopher Tusubira, incredulously, "we are learning."

Men, in general, approve of their wives working with SHARE. They're earning money, and their husbands know where they are. It's often the men who inquire about membership for their wives. The women agree that being working women doesn't directly empower them in their homes, but there is no doubt that having money gives you independence, and men will respect you more because of it. And AIDS? Well, there was a woman who had it. You used to meet her at the water pump. People didn't speak to her, though.

Two women describe typical days in their lives. Guljerbi from India gets up before the sun to draw water, clean round the house, get the breakfast, take the children to school and then walk a mile and a half to the center, going home for lunch in the middle of the day to prepare food for the family. Cristina Cavalcanti from Brazil works from home using telephone, fax and E-mail. Her three-year-old daughter Carmen is at nursery from

11:00 a.m. to 6:00 p.m., and has lunch there. Her husband looks after Carmen when Cristina is traveling. The contrast between the two women's lives could hardly be more stark.

Looking back on this week in Vellore, with all its fun and tears and long, intense discussions, its insights and parties and sudden friendships, this is the occasion I regard as the real revelation experience. We left the women of SHARE having learned more about the reality of Indian women, yes, but also with a new sense of wonder about the world that looks so different depending on the cultural spectacles through which you see it. And also with a new sense of the privilege of encounter with people of other cultures, and how much of yourself you have to risk in order to hear what they are saying.

## LOVE STORY

Jim and Helen Worth come from Portville, New York, in the USA. Jim is a retired machinist, now a volunteer for a driving service for old people, and also for younger people who have lost their licenses. Helen retired from teaching in 1988 and now works with the Methodist AIDS task force. They have three grown-up children and ten grandchildren.

Helen became infected with HIV in 1981 from a blood transfusion given during surgery. She remembers the years between 1981 and 1988, when she was diagnosed positive, as ones when she was constantly tired, so tired, she says, that she could have lain down on the sidewalk and gone to sleep. "Teachers are always tired," said the doctor. "Take iron tablets." Then one day, urged by her students, she agreed to give blood. Within a day or two an envelope arrived with the address of the blood transfusion service on the outside. Assuming it was routine, she put it aside. Finding it lying around one day, she was about to throw it away unopened. "Oh, I'd better look at it," she thought. Inside was a letter informing her that she was infected with the virus that causes AIDS, and would she please ring the transfusion center as soon as possible. She remembers the way the voice on the end of the phone changed when she said her name. "Holy cow," said the voice, "it's her!"

"Go to an STD clinic at a city far away from here," she was told, "and they'll give you a number." She remembers, as if it was yesterday, the rage she felt. "I want to go to my own doctor, in my own town, using my own name," she said. "And if I'm told I can't, then I'll go to the center of town and stand there with a megaphone and tell everybody I'm infected and how you're treating me." It was the first of many victories.

Jim's first thought when he knew was "What's *she* been up to?" His second was "What did *I* get up to when I was in the Navy?" But Jim, miraculously, tested negative. They talk about the time of coming to terms with the infection, about Helen's struggle with the school board, about her new life working in adult education.

When she was first diagnosed, Helen's T-cell count was 110. Feeling better as a result of AZT, determined not to give in to the virus, she worked incredibly hard at what she still saw as her "real job," where her heart was, and got home dead tired. In the meantime, Jim did the housework and shopped for food; ferried her here and there to consultations, committees, etc. Jim, she now sees, was getting the scraps of her life. Always a quiet man, he was getting quieter and lonelier as time went by.

"And I never noticed," says Helen. It is clear to her now that, however horrible it is to be living with HIV, the role of the carer is even more difficult. He or she—and it's usually she—is not supported in the same way, and doesn't get the attention the infected person gets.

As well as getting quieter, Jim says he was also getting angry. But Helen was always out and about, speaking to groups, going to meetings. Jim's a quiet man, she thought. He won't enjoy it. He's better off at home. And always, when she got home, she was exhausted. Frightened by his rising rage, Jim took his clothes and moved to an upstairs bedroom. And then came the sugges-tion that Helen should join the WCC group in Beijing. She had not been well, was not really fit to travel long distances alone. Jim tried to dissuade her, but she was determined. Eventually, "Do what you like, Helen," said Jim. "You always do anyway."

And the letters kept coming from WCC. Beijing? India? What difference did it make? It occurred to Helen that they were near divorce. Then her (woman) doctor said to her, "Why don't you take Jim with you?" "Oh, I couldn't," said Helen. "He'd hate it." But Jim, when she asked him, said, "Fine!" She describes those two weeks as a time of faxes and visas and tickets and scratching round for money to pay for it, and all the time Jim getting happier and happier. "Dad's more excited than you are, Mom," said her daughter. The day they left home, Helen turned to her husband. "I'll never go away again without you," she said.

In Vellore, on the night before our meeting begins, we play a game. In it, everybody has to pretend to be an animal, then look for a mate of the same species. Jim has been cast as a crocodile— an impossible role to play with any dignity. Watching Jim wallowing there on the floor, his arms turned to great flailing jaws, Helen suddenly sees him with new eyes. He's loving this, she thinks, wonderingly.

The day comes when she is to give her presentation to the seminar. "Why don't you go someplace else while I speak?" she asks. "Fine," he says. The picture of the laughing crocodile comes into her mind. "Or you could do it with me," she says. "Why *shouldn't* we do it together?"

And so they do. Two grandparents, both in their sixties: Helen, vital and articulate; Jim, shy, unused to talking in public at all, let alone sharing feelings and private experiences with strangers. Together they tell the story of their personal road to Vellore. When they finish, they turn and hold each other gently.

Nobody speaks. Nobody is *able* to speak. We are all too aware of the great and private privilege of being witnesses to a story of love.

## PLATFORM OF ACTION

The week in Vellore was not without its problems. Rebecca had flu; a scorpion wandered into Caroline's bedroom on the first night. Florence, who has AIDS and who had never been out of Uganda before, was ill for much of the time. News came from Maureen's husband of an impending hurricane in Antigua, and then nothing; telephone lines down, nothing reported on the BBC World Service. We had a fax from Marisa in Papua New Guinea. The day before, on their way to the center, three of her social workers were gang-raped, so she couldn't come away just now.

People disagreed with each other, sometimes passionately. There were the long, sleepy, perspiring afternoons when the fans whirred gently, the voices drifted peacefully in and out of focus.

It is infinitely challenging to present your work in this kind of international context, have it reflected back at you from other cultural standpoints, and to struggle towards some common mind about philosophy, theology and practical possibilities. It's impossible here to do justice to what happened in Vellore, or not without writing out, word for word, much of the extraordinarily rich debate which unrolled, day after day in the course of the meeting.

So I'm not going to try. My task has been to reflect back what happened at this seminar in such a way that it means something to people who were not present. But it's left me dissatisfied, because it's meant that I haven't adequately acknowledged the people whose thoughts my own comments represent. This is their book, really, not mine, coming out of their lives and experiences, their views and understandings.

As a group whose mandate was to look at women and health in relation to the challenge of HIV/AIDS, our final task was to put together some recommendations for future action. This message, unanimously agreed, turned out eventually to be a challenge to the churches. The Platform of Action itself is reproduced on pages xiv-xvi. The thinking behind it, hotly debated in Vellore, forms the subject matter of the final chapters of this book.

# 7

## SONS OF MARY,
## DAUGHTERS OF EVE

### MATER ET MAGISTRA

Participants in the Vellore consultation were unanimous about one thing—that the experience of living or working with HIV/AIDS had in some way been a formative one. It had broken into our existing preconceptions, had disturbed our moral and spiritual assumptions. Within that experience, we felt, a challenge is contained, not just to us as individuals, but to our churches, and to people of faith in general.

The church has a good record in caring for people with AIDS. In doing so, churches, mission hospitals and other Christian organizations often faced with courage the ignorance, fear and prejudice with which—in the early days—people reacted to the virus and those who were living with it. In many parts of the world, Christian groups have treated and cared for people living with and affected by the virus. This caring church is Latin American liberation theologian Leonardo Boff's "mater et magistra," mother and teacher, exercising its Christian concern for the world around it.

When it comes to prevention, churches—in common with others—have operated first and foremost in the belief that greater understanding of the facts will lead to behavior change in individuals. But what kinds of behavior change? The standard answers are abstinence and monogamy, as the most reliable forms of "safe sex" available, in relation to which it has often been said that the virus's most important lesson is a moral one, directed at individuals whom it calls back to a sexual morality that they have abandoned. Where monogamy and abstinence have proved impossible, churches vary in the forms of preventive behavior they are willing to sanction; but by far the most widely accepted one is, of course, the use of the male condom.

The powerlessness of many women when it comes to negotiating safe sex has been repeatedly stressed in the previous pages. Abstinence? You don't become a mother, nor may you remain a wife for long, by abstaining. Monogamy? Many women *are* monogamous; they may be infected, without knowing it, by unfaithful or drug-injecting partners. Condoms? Just try persuading a man to use a condom when he doesn't want to. Negotiation with your partner? If cultural bias against open discussion of sexual matters co-exists with the cultural expectation that women are "innocent" in these matters, then how does *either* partner initiate such a discussion, let alone the female one?

With all that is said and written about HIV/AIDS, why this bizarre failure to recognize the truth as seen through the eyes of women?

So the main challenge of the Ecumenical Platform of Action hammered out and unanimously agreed in Vellore is to the churches, which have not, in general, registered the relevance to their own cultures and traditions of the message coming from individuals and communities who have genuinely faced up to the existence of AIDS. The message coming from the work described in these pages is that HIV/AIDS carries an overwhelming judgment on the churches themselves.

## BLESS ME, FATHER

Where the church itself is organized in a patriarchal way, it provides a powerful model of the kind of society which makes the subordination of women an entry point for HIV. This is not just another call for women's ordination. It's a call for us to become aware of the whole male-dominated infrastructure of bureaucracy and liturgy, of theologies professing to take the world seriously but actually speaking only from male experience, of patriarchal models of mission and ministry, and of fundamentalist theologies that seek refuge from the complexities of today's world in so-called "traditional" values which have nothing to do with current reality.

In many churches, of course, women can now be encountered within the corridors of power. But even where this is the case, the culture in which that encounter takes place, and the assumptions that underlie that culture, will probably be male. The world seen through the experience of women is quite simply not admissible here, except maybe via "the women's desk," which may have little contact with other departments.

Women working in the church often find themselves colluding with this state of affairs. They may consciously play the male game, as a strategy for furthering a favorite project. Because they fear being cast as single-issue people, they may fail to challenge ignorant or gender-biased assumptions. I am guilty of both these things, although I know that in doing so, I make it increasingly unlikely that the male cultural norms will ever be challenged.

Assumptions that equity has been achieved may persist in the face of overwhelming evidence to the contrary. For instance, in one of the Latin American countries I visited in 1995, contraceptive advice is not available at all to poor women except through certain Protestant church agencies. The Roman Catholic Church's influence on government is too strong. While I and a (male) colleague were there, the rector of the ecumenical (but mainly Protestant) theological seminary kindly invited Roman Catholic and Protestant church leaders to meet us. It was an interesting meeting, and we were most warmly received. Fifteen men were present and (apart from myself) one woman. "Women have family responsibilities in the late afternoon," I was told, understandingly. I asked later why they had decided not to go ahead with a staff appointment for a feminist theologian. Was it finance? Conflicting priorities? Well, you know, I was told, there really is no problem here now for women. It's pointless politicizing them to fight other people's battles—ones which, in this country, have already been won. To my everlasting shame, I was too well-mannered to challenge this extraordinary statement.

In São Paulo, I spent a day with a group of academic feminist theologians. They were mourning the departure of one of their members, the Brazilian theologian Ivone Gebara, stripped of her job as head of a religious community and sent by her superiors for retraining in Europe. Was that because of her stance on abortion and contraception? I asked. Not really, they thought. The real issue had been her theology, her questioning of the patriarchal structure of the Roman Catholic Church. It's often said that liberation theology in Brazil is in the doldrums because of the new economic order, and the changing power relationship with Rome. But they now believe the liberation theology agenda was always destined to founder. In interpreting the world from the standpoint of the poor and oppressed, it has consistently failed to address issues of patriarchy in the church itself. And until these are addressed, there will be no real liberation in any society whose members trust the church to be a sign and a foretaste of God's kingdom. The God of liberation theology, say Latin American women theologians, has come to possess all the characteristics of a left-wing white man.

On the wider, global scale—as third-world woman theologians in particular have recently observed—patriarchy in the church mirrors and endorses the capitalist ethic which keeps half the world poor and powerless. Colonialist models of partnership, and the catastrophic effects of the dependence syndrome they have created, have been replaced by the parallel imperialism of the new economic order. Seduced, as we are, into a conviction that there is no alternative, it is easy to become deaf to the warnings of the environmentalists. And yet this same mindset underwrites and endorses ecological destruction. As US Roman Catholic theologian Rosemary Radford Ruether puts it, "He (man) rapes (destroys) her (the planet)."

In denying the right of women to name their experience, to describe and own their own sexuality, the voice of the virus echoes that of the shanty town and the "silent spring": that capitalism and patriarchy, together, have turned domination into a paradigm. And churches have not just "let it happen": they've provided a model for it. Addressing institutional patriarchy is no longer just a matter of justice. It's the condition of the church's commitment to life itself.

## SCANDAL TO THE JEWS, FOLLY TO THE GREEKS?

Jesus claimed that he had come so that his followers might have life, and have it more abundantly. In a time of AIDS, what might this mean?

It is a central claim of Christian tradition that Jesus first shows us how to live, and then helps us to do it correctly. Cristina Gutierrez looks at the story of the woman with the bent back (Luke 13:10-17). Preaching in the synagogue, Jesus sees this woman, calls out to her, and she is healed. The woman "glorifies

God" for her transformation, but the synagogue staff are furious. People may come to be healed six days a week, they say, but not on the Sabbath. "You are being inconsistent," says Jesus. "You let out your ox and ass on the Sabbath, and you give them water, otherwise they might die. Are you saying that the Law values human life lower than that of animals? This woman," he says, "is a daughter of Abraham." Abraham, the unlikely patriarch of questionable morals who is entrusted by God with the future of God's people. Abraham, who symbolizes new beginnings, who walks into God's future not knowing where he is going, armed only with faith in God's promises and his own God-given capacity to fulfill them.

In this case, then, the "law" has become an opponent of the divine project of giving more abundant life. For Jesus, it seems, life is to be ranked *above* morality, or as offering a new and different criterion upon which moralities might be based.

What, then, is the place of moral teaching in the gospels? The usual answer is that the morality of the Pharisees was wrong because it ignored the *spirit* of the Law, but the morality of the church—which got this different set of rules from Jesus—is right. But many modern ethicists, their Christian formation rooted in the assumption that Jesus' *teachings* somehow provide a blueprint for Christian living, describe the unnerving experience of coming to realize just how difficult this belief is to maintain. Because if you look at Jesus' *life* as well as just his teachings, it is clear that in many ways it was nothing short of scandalous when he was alive, and would certainly have been considered so today. He was often angry, sometimes unsociable. He was rude to his mother, and didn't wash his hands before meals. He preferred the company of bent financiers and loose women to that of respectable people. The evangelical British theologian Michael Vasey has recently suggested that the gospel Jesus would have felt quite at home in a gay bar. His feckless troop of followers walked out on family and jobs—valuable assets like fishing boats included—in order to join him. They sponged ruthlessly on whoever would feed them. They were encouraged to leave, even to *hate* father and mother, to let the dead bury the dead.

In his final journey to Jerusalem, Jesus seems deliberately to have courted his violent and terrible death, though in great agony of mind about it, and left his followers lost and confused, with no real brief as to how they should now behave. Hardly responsible behavior in a leader.

Yet in spite of all this evidence, the disciples seem still to have believed that the Jesus kingdom was to be recognizably similar to the structures they were familiar with. Only days before his death, they were still arguing about where each of them would be in the hierarchy of this "kingdom," and about its rules. And Christian moralists have persisted, over the centuries, in suggesting that Jesus' main message was about morality, that Christian living is a matter of following rules about what you do and don't do, and that church hierarchies know best.

The Danish philosopher Kierkegaard realized that "If morality is given such predominance, then ethics has become God." The morality preached by the church may prevent people from grappling with the real gospel evidence of the life of Jesus. If Jesus is God incarnate, then his life must contain vital clues about what is most valuable, the values we in our own lives should strive to embody. If Jesus' life contains mess and pain, and a love-hate relationship with established religious authorities and their certainties, then why should we expect ours to be full of order, calm, and unqualified acceptance of the certainties of the church?

The German theologian Dietrich Bonhoeffer claims that the Pharisee, far from being the stereotypical hypocrite that Christian prejudice has made him, is in fact that wholly admirable person, known to us all, who sees everything in terms of the knowledge of good and evil. He suggests that in "knowing good and evil," and making that knowledge our god, we alienate ourselves from the potentially chaotic experience of knowing and following the living God. Christian discipleship, he claims, involves *unlearning* that "good and evil" knowledge, which was the primal cause of our alienation from Eden. If, in Adam, we die (that is, if we worship the rules rather than God), then in Christ we may now be made alive. Not good, not moral, but alive. It's not that the rules are necessarily wrong (although they may be), says the living Christ. It's just that if that's where you're looking for God, then you're looking in the wrong place.

Peter Harvey, in *The Morals of Jesus*, suggests that cultural paradigms of sanity may operate in a parallel way. The ego encases itself in a shell of certainties, all the more impregnable because they embody the surrounding cultural mores that we

convince ourselves are the basis of our survival. In losing that
"sanity," we become open to rebirth into truth, and love, and life.
Mad as it seems, says Harvey, Jesus' final journey to Jerusalem to
an apparently pointless death constitutes the shedding of the
cloak of sanity by which we make sense of our lives. Jerusalem,
and all it stood for, had to be faced. Sanity, morals, the hopes of
the disciples—they counted for nothing. This was what the
journey of his life was *for.*

This road to Jerusalem is a fearful road to tread, though.
Because if I turn my back on the rules, on the "sanity" that provides my survival mechanisms, on the priorities of my family and
friends, what am I left with? Harvey quotes the Welsh poet R.S.
Thomas, writing about Morgan, the minister from the Welsh hills,
obsessed by the sinful behavior of his dwindling congregation:

> He never listened to the hills'
> Music calling to the hushed
> Music within; but let his mind
> Fester with brooding on the sly
> Infirmities of the hill people.
> The pus conspired with the old
> Infection lurking in his breast.

Morgan was imagining that God's message to the world was a
set of narrowly moralistic and conventional codes. He was therefore failing to encounter the living God in the mysteries of his
own heart, the realities of the world around. He was interpreting
the world, for himself and his "flock," in terms of the life-denying
rules of the "grown-up" world. But entry to God's future, says
Jesus, depends on becoming like little children, nurturing our
capacity for experiencing the magic and the joy of life, safe-
guarding Eden from the wiles of the serpent who would
convince us that the road to salvation is defined by the knowledge of good and evil.

## JUDGE NOT THAT YE BE NOT JUDGED

A fashionable insult in church circles today is to say that somebody is "judgmental." It's a word you only use about other
people; nobody will ever admit to being judgmental themselves.
The gospels are full of warnings about judging other people's

failures, and Jesus' condemnation of people who criticized other people's faults while ignoring "the plank in their own eyes." These are surprisingly combined with remarks that suggest that Jesus is wanting to *toughen up* some prohibitions, notably those against anger and lustful thoughts. Peter Harvey points out that these remarks are made in situations where the detail of the law is what matters. What Jesus is really saying, suggests Harvey, is "If you must think in that way, then at least do so consistently and across the board. If, for instance, you are hell-bent on draconian measures against the adulterer, then why not show comparable severity to the would-be adulterer? You must follow your logic through to the bitter end."

It wasn't that Jesus was commending anger, or adultery. It seems to have been people who judge others without applying the same criteria to themselves who made Jesus so cross, because it represented an attempt to manipulate divine mercy. He talked about hypocrisy far more often than he talked about justice. The letter to the Romans makes the same point: that in setting up man-made laws by which we judge others instead of trusting in the limitless grace of God, we are in effect replacing God's laws with our own. The Gentiles, who follow comparable rules because "the requirements of the law are written in their hearts," are in the same boat even if they do not have the Torah, because similar "natural" laws are written on their hearts.

The trouble is that "hypocrisy" is another word we only ever use about other people. So why not try using the word "inconsistent" instead? Because over matters concerning sexuality, most churches are riddled with inconsistency. The following examples, in one form or another, are repeated all over the world, though I have listed the countries where I can name a particular source.

(i) A commercial sex worker is socially ostracized. The family man who hired her remains a pillar of his church (Thailand, India, USA, Ghana).

(ii) Because of a church's proclaimed belief in the sanctity of life, abortion is not permitted. The church's attitude changes after the baby is born: unmarried mothers or mothers who have too many children have "made their own beds" and must cope as best they can (Argentina, USA).

(iii) A priest preaches about his church's ban on artificial means of contraception. Nobody argues. The congregation has made up its own mind; most of the sexually active members of the congregation use one form of contraception or another (all over the world).

(iv) "The church has always had a problem with me because of my homosexuality. It's amazing how they love me now I've got AIDS" (UK).

(v) The church stipulates celibate male clergy; diocesan funds are secretly paid out to mistresses and children of (still practicing) priests (Ireland, Italy).

When Jesus pointed to the moral inconsistency of the religious establishment, he wasn't just having another go at the Pharisee, that stereotypical Jewish fall-guy of Christian tradition. He was drawing attention to a basic human tendency to project blame onto others, and to sweep our own shortcomings under the carpet. But Christian tradition has somehow set the Pharisee up as "the other," and become blind to the fact that the churches themselves are guilty of exactly the same inconsistencies, creating cultures within which individual church-goers become convinced that they, too, are more moral than others, just because they go to church. "Thank God I am not as others are."

It is the experience of many church-goers that churches tend to place upon them the onus of being "holier than thou" in terms of sexuality. In some religious traditions, the ritual purification of women after childbirth still occurs. In the majority of church cultures, homosexuality, polygamy, divorce, extra-marital relationships, abortion and illegitimacy are all things that happen "out there." Agonized repentance is the passport back into the fold, concealment the condition for flourishing within it. Thus churches have created a mythical culture for themselves, and have effectively demonized whole areas of human experience. Victims of rape and sexual violence speak of their churches as shrinking from the knowledge of what has happened. As a result, it's almost impossible to talk about these things in most churches, except in the hushed and contrite terms of one who is saying "I am unclean."

## DAUGHTERS OF EVE . . .

The church is part of the world. But it is also called to tell the truth *about* the world in so far as it is able, and to embody in its own life the spirit of God's future. This chapter is an attempt to see why AIDS/HIV constitutes such a specific ethical challenge to the churches.

The North American theologian Walter Wink spells out the importance of "naming the powers"—those invisible forces, so much part of the consciousness that they are like the air we breathe, which ring-fence our institutions and protect them from harm. In the case of the church, patriarchy must be regarded as one of those powers. So is the obsession with rules. But are there others?

It is always threatening for those who are inside a culture to examine its most deeply-held assumptions, and attitudes to sexuality, in particular, tend to be culture-specific. It's the nature of institutions to protect themselves from knowledge that threatens their structures and hierarchies. Such knowledge may be outlawed, and individuals who give voice to it from within may be forced to leave.

Cristina Gutierrez, whose study of poor women in Argentina is discussed in Chapter 4, recognizes that the churches have particular difficulties in coping with issues of women's subordination. Their theology of what it means to be a woman is underpinned by two immensely powerful female symbols—the figures of Eve, the first woman, and Mary the mother of Jesus.

First of all, Eve. There are two versions, in Genesis, of her creation. The earlier one has Adam and Eve made jointly in the image of God—a man-and-woman team. The second reading has Eve formed out of Adam's rib, as a complement and a companion for him.

But it's from the story of The Fall that the negative power of the Eve-symbol derives. Here Eve becomes the temptress, open to the blandishments of the serpent, wrapping poor upstanding Adam in her seductive wiles. In fact, this character assassination is not born out by a careful reading of Genesis 3. God's attitude to Adam and Eve is of sadness. Now that they have eaten of the tree of knowledge of good and evil, Eden *cannot* be theirs; going back to Kierkegaard's and Bonhoeffer's interpretations (p. 81 above), the temptation is to see everything in terms of a rigid moral code that protects us from knowledge of the living God, and from the Eden which, as children of God, is our inheritance. God's sharpest anger is reserved for the serpent, whose lies and manipulation are the real source of humankind's alienation from God's self. And yet, as the South Korean theologian Chung Hyun Kyung pointed out on reading an early draft of this chapter, the serpent is also part of God's creation.

Ivone Gebara writes, "It is from the relationship with Eve that the denial of Eve emerges, it is from the fear of Eve's power that the struggle for the denial of Eve's power is born, it is from the fascination of Eve that anti-feminisms are born . . ." Eve, says Gebara, has a vital energy which can "break the desired harmony, cause chaos and confusion, attract and confuse without reason, and finally act as a denial of human reason." Her excess power therefore needs restraining. Adam, it seems, has been partly forgiven for his part in the Fall. Eve, on the other hand, continues to be blamed. "All women," says Gebara, "are Eve and are responsible for the initial corruption of humanity."

The place of the Eve myth in relation to other contemporary anthropologies has been well documented. So has the sociological position of women in Jewish society after the establishment of the monarchy, which might have sanctioned it then. Today, the actual figure of Eve has largely disappeared from our consciousness, although the myth has survived the context for which it was needed. In terms of the iconography of our faith, it has become embodied in the ontological reality of "woman." In response, Judeo-Christian tradition has created "psychological, social, political, religious and cultural mechanisms in order to avoid freeing the power of Eve—mechanisms which have come, over the millennia, to appear to be God's plan, or natural law."

There is an abundance of gospel evidence that Jesus did not accept the invisibility of women within his own culture. As Gutierrez points out in her study of Luke 13, the bent woman healed on the Sabbath was referred to by Jesus as a "daughter of Abraham"—a reference to the Messianic role of the one who carries on the promise. The redemption of Adam must include the redemption of Eve. Part of the restoration of Eden must be the restoration of women to their proper place in it.

## . . . AND SONS OF MARY

If Eve embodies this fearful power, what of that other icon, Mary the mother of Jesus?

I am writing this section in a quiet, warm room, at the turn of the year, in the Anglican Community of St. Mary the Virgin. For this order, I asked Sr. Margaret Elizabeth, what is the key message of Mary? Being open to the reality of the world, she said, and to the presence of God in it, while accepting that we can never understand the full mystery of God incarnate. Every day, the nuns say, "At all times and in all places, I am the handmaid of the Lord; be it unto me according to thy word."

The Bible contains many models of womanhood: Sarah, Hannah, Ruth; Rahab, prostitute and freedom fighter; Mary Magdelene, whom Jesus loved. But it's Mary the virgin, mother of God, who has exercised this great power over the imaginations of Christians and non-Christians for almost two thousand years. She's undoubtedly the most painted woman in the world. She's queen of heaven, she's our mother, she's the one Christians turn to, men as well as women when, failing to find what they need in our all-male Trinity, they need a woman to pray to. She's the one who worries about the wine running out at Cana; she's the one who weeps at the foot of the cross. She's the role model who was held up to me, a plump and solemn nine-year-old Protestant, at my Catholic convent school in Cape Town. We must keep our thoughts and bodies pure, be little brides of Christ, like holy Mary. Bride-of-Christ Mary; mother Mary; virgin Mary. All those things? How odd, I thought. Even at the age of nine.

Christ, says the Mary story, is conceived without any of the messy business of sex, born without blood or pain. The early fathers believed that Jesus was conceived via Mary's ear, which—Jesus being the word of God—is not an unreasonable assumption. The Irish Catholic theologian Anne Thurston points out that while there is plenty of blood and agony at the crucifixion, descriptions of Jesus' birth have neither. Pictures of the nativity tend to move straight from the journey to Bethlehem, via "no room at the inn," to Mary and Joseph kneeling tidily by the manger waiting for their visitors.

How convenient! The Eve in us is conquered; indeed Mary is often pictured standing soulfully staring into space, her delicate foot on the neck of a writhing serpent. But Eve is redeemed only to be replaced by another impossible symbol. Little Christian girls, for evermore, are confronted with a model of womanhood they can never hope to live up to, and church-going Christians are encouraged in the fantasy that Jesus came into being without blood or sex, so really good women don't have either. The "churching" of women after childbirth is supposed to cleanse them of all that mess and make them fit, once more, to come into the presence of God.

But it's not only women whose assumptions about their own sexuality have been formed by the polarization of Eve-and-Mary in Christian culture. Male images of sexuality are affected too. On the one hand *I'm* Eve, which means *you* are filled with self-loathing for being seduced by me; on the other I'm Mary, turning every act of intercourse into a (more or less controlled) rape. Either way, sex is shameful; either way, you lose.

Eve or Mary? Woman is the defiler or the undefiled, the whore who exercises this terrifying, irresistible power over men and leads them to acts of shame, or the unapproachable virgin of whom the most that lustful man can expect is that she will briefly have compassion on him. Think this is fiction? My friends and I hadn't a clue what sex would be like, but we knew, by the time we were teenagers, that no man would ever respect us if we seemed to want it, that the way to make them marry us was to play hard-to-get, and that nice girls never *ever* initiate anything sexual. But we knew the Eve-like characters, too: well, everyone did. They were the ones who egged men on, and let them "do things." *They,* said our mothers, would *never* get decent men.

Sharing these experiences with women friends from South America, South Africa and India, I am surprised find how universal they are. And with young women, too. With so much sexual behavior around in magazines, films and TV, one might expect things to be different today. But they're not. On the one hand, the media trade romantic illusions of beautiful people in exotic places who bear no relationship to the real-life struggles of young people developing their sexuality, and just serve to make them feel inadequate. On the other hand, they stoke other fantasies with scenes of explicit sex and violence that degrade women in ways that young people may come to think of as normal. And the saddest thing of all is this: that with all the paper, screen and celluloid sex that goes on in the media, there is considerable evidence that for the majority of families, in all parts of the world but particularly in parts of Asia, talk about the *reality* of sex is virtually taboo.

Which brings me back to Luke 13 and the woman with the bent back. In common with the rest of us, this nameless woman is neither Eve nor Mary, neither vamp nor virgin. She is the third member in the unholy trinity of women: she is the victim. Therefore she is nobody. It is to this woman that Jesus reaches out on the Sabbath and offers the gift of life.

I'm not saying the churches are responsible for the ills of the world. What I am saying is that their iconography of women bears little or no relation to reality, and that they are, on the whole, extremely bad at helping Christians to own their sexual experience. The churches, far from encouraging a more open and truthful approach to sexual matters, have become, for Christians, part of the problem. We encourage unrealistic images of women. We collude with the illusion that Christians are different from other people in matters of sexual behavior and sexual orientation. We fail to challenge the discomfort church people feel in talking about these matters. And in these ways, we reinforce existing societal factors that prevent young people, in particular, from learning to negotiate safe sex at a time when that lesson may be a condition of survival.

## NOW YOU SEE IT, NOW YOU DON'T

The WCC's Seventh Assembly was held in Canberra, Australia, in 1991. The following quotation comes from an address given by Korean theologian Chung Hyun Kyung.

> For me, the image of the Holy Spirit comes from the image of Kwan In. She is venerated as goddess of compassion and wisdom by East Asian women's popular religiosity. She is a *bodhisattva,* an enlightened being. She can go into Nirvana any time she wants to, but refuses to go into Nirvana by herself. Her compassion for all suffering living beings makes her stay in this world enabling other living beings to achieve enlightenment... Perhaps this might also be a feminine image of the Christ who is the first-born among us, one who goes before and brings others with her?

I am grateful to Alison Webster for her comments on the reactions to this presentation. There was apparently an uproar among some delegates, notably white male Westerners and those representing the Orthodox churches. The complaint was that

Chung was being "syncretistic," a term that refers to the mixing of socio-cultural and/or religious beliefs which previously existed independently. Originally used positively, to mean "a prudent alliance," the word "syncretistic" has become something of a term of abuse in theological circles in recent years. In this case, the suggestion was that while her critics subscribed to some "pure" form of Christianity, Chung had developed an unacceptable hybrid in which Christian beliefs were combined with traditions and religious beliefs of her own culture.

What was not recognized, Webster comments, was that the faith of the accusers was just as syncretistic. White male Westerners, for instance, subscribe to a faith which is heavily influenced by western capitalism and Victorian morality. When a third-world woman brings traditional insights to bear on Christianity, she's being syncretistic; when rich white western men draw on the political and economic thought forms that underpin the domination of the Third World, what emerges is normative Christianity. Webster applies the same insight to Christian debates about polygamy in African countries. The western nuclear family, which developed in a very different cultural and political context, has become the normative "genuinely Christian" pattern of family life, while the churches anxiously debate whether "polygamous lifestyles" should be allowed.

These two examples make the same point: that the boundaries of acceptable Christian belief are defined, usually by men, in particular contexts and for particular political reasons. The reasons are then forgotten, the boundaries become normative, and are then applied in situations for which they are inappropriate.

This chapter has looked at some of the invisible "powers" identified at the Vellore consultation, that underpin churches' responses to HIV/AIDS, and make it so difficult for them to face the connection between the transmission of the virus and the subordination of women. The final chapter will look at some approaches that open up when these powers have been exposed and recognized for what they are.

# 8

# LOVE IN THE TIME OF AIDS

**LOVE STORY**

Yupa Suta's husband was a leader in a local church in Chiang Mai, Thailand. He was a good man, says Yupa, and a good husband. But church business took him away, sometimes for weeks at a time. When he started to be sick a lot, Yupa thought he was just exhausted, but the doctor suggested a blood test. Afterwards, he came home and said nothing. But Yupa knew something was wrong and said so. "Supposing I had AIDS," he asked, "what would you do?" Yupa said she loved him and would stay with him whatever happened. "Go and have a blood test," he said to her, "and then we'll talk."

Yupa found that she was HIV-positive a few days before Mother's Day, which in Thailand falls on August 12. On August 13, returning from his mother's home, her husband became very sick indeed. Yupa cared for him, cleaned him, washed his soiled bedding. An active man, he found it difficult to be bedridden. Sometimes too exhausted to walk, she crawled into bed and slept with him at nights. Just before he died, he had a week in hospital. Then the doctor asked, "Are you ready to take your husband home?" "Are *you* ready, ready to meet God?" Yupa asked her husband. "I'm ready," he answered.

On his last night, he seemed better, happier. They talked till 2:00 in the morning, about what she would do, how she would cope. He wouldn't let her out of his sight, even to get a glass of water. Normally, each of them had their own blanket. When it was time to sleep, he asked if they could share the same blanket, if she would hold him till he died and not leave him. When Yupa woke in the morning, she realized she had done just that.

Yupa's story is the story of hundreds of thousands of women the world over. She is infected by the man she loves, the man who loves her, the man she goes on loving. She cares for him until he dies in her arms. Now she is alone, with the world to face, and her own future.

From having been a respectable person, a church leader's wife, Yupa became an object of curiosity—a woman with AIDS, who would soon die. Her mother-in-law would introduce her as "My son's wife who has AIDS." Eventually, she moved out and lived alone, waiting to die, wishing it would happen soon. "I was living like a demented person," she says. "I neglected myself, my appearance." And then one day she met a group of people who understood what it was all about, who gave her good advice, who accepted her for what she was. She started taking exercise, eating properly, resting. She did "spiritual and mental exercise." She realized that she had to take responsibility for herself. She realized, she says, that God is with her day and night, always has been and always will be.

Yupa became a volunteer with the HIV/AIDS support group at the Church of Christ in Thailand health promotion unit. "I now feel so loved, cherished and valued," she says. "Life has so much meaning for me now. The work I do is important. It helps me and is a source of strength every minute, every day. For me, every day and every night, every minute has its meaning and value, its purpose. I believe that every person living with HIV/AIDS loves his or her life as much as I do. Nobody gets HIV on purpose."

## LIFE AFTER HIV

Yupa's story is a story about one woman. It might equally have been Shunila in Dakar, Florence in Kagoma, Shanti in Vellore or Martha in London. All of them say the same thing. HIV comes out of the blue. At first you don't believe it; life goes on as usual around you, but for you the world has changed. At first you think you can hide the fact that you are HIV+, live as if nothing had happened. But as, inevitably, more and more people find out, you may lose job or family. You will certainly lose friends.

People don't want you around. It's not just that they're afraid of physical infection, though that's part of it. The virus makes them nervous in less tangible but more far-reaching ways than that. It's almost as if it shows them their own vulnerability, their own mortality, and they don't want to know about it. The fact that the virus is most often sexually transmitted makes people feel particularly vulnerable. It's an admission of the sexuality of the infected person, a confirmation of the secret fear that sex really is something nasty and dangerous, an endorsement of all the moral ambiguity people may feel about their own sexuality but don't acknowledge.

Most churches are not safe places for people with HIV/AIDS. Yupa and others have spoken of their despair when they discovered they had become outcasts from the old world they'd occupied before. They speak of the people who helped them "realize that I have to be responsible for myself." They speak of emerging into a new kind of living, the feeling of being accepted, and accepting themselves, in ways they've never experienced before; a sense of the preciousness of human life, the value of human love, the importance of living and loving to the full; a new understanding of life's meaning.

People with AIDS are left with few illusions about the facade of normality and respectability that people mistake for reality. This facade hides fear. AIDS exposes that fear. Maybe, says the virus, this ordered, predictable life you live is not the norm. If love can do this to people, anything can happen.

In a respectable church-going group, people will prefer to pretend that it wasn't really love at all. It was just sex, just lust. Just sin. To be infected with HIV is to be guilty. There are "innocent" victims, of course, like Yupa. But she will be assumed to be contaminated, too, with more than the virus. She is connected by marriage with someone who's "sinned" and, sad though one is for Yupa, she's placed herself in that universe of chaos where respectable people don't go. Like homosexual men. Like people who inject narcotics. AIDS is something you get when you step outside the magic circle where people know what the rules are, and where those of us who obey them will, by definition, be OK.

We are, of course, compassionate people, we respectable ones. The rules of our bit of the magic circle say we must care for the sick, the dying, the orphans, the widows, even if they have broken the rules and put themselves beyond the pale. If pushed, we would say that of course we (who know the rules) all bend them from time to time. But we do it with circumspection. We do it carefully. Because the most important rule of the magic circle is, "Thou shalt not be found out." To be infected with HIV is to be found out. To be infected with HIV is to surrender your membership of the magic circle. To be outside the magic circle is to be less than fully human.

In all this, where might Jesus have been? I have suggested that the thing that drove people wild with irritation about Jesus was that he wasn't at all interested in the rules. He wasn't mixing with tax collectors and prostitutes because he was sorry for them, or wanted to "convert" them, whatever that might have meant. He did it because he was welcome there. He was happy. The magic circle of respectability meant nothing to him, and people could have coped with that if they'd been able to think of him as a sinner. I mean, that's where sinners belong, don't they, outside the magic circle?

Jesus made respectable people uncomfortable. Like Yupa, it therefore had to be possible to define him as one who is unclean, or contaminated by sin. And so they set all those traps for him. If he'd fallen into them, they'd have felt OK about themselves again, order would have been restored, and they might not have needed to kill him. As it was, he broke the rules of the magic circle, but at the same time defied all attempts to prove him sinful. By constantly pointing out the inconsistencies that enabled people to continue in membership, Jesus challenged the whole system and all of us who belong to it. And so he had to be got rid of.

## CHALLENGING THE MARKET

"Social injustice, and the legalized inequality that produces poverty, are basic factors in the risk of HIV infection," says Cristina Gutierrez. This is not just true at the local level. An analysis of the resources going into the prevention and cure of AIDS shows that 94 percent are spent in the developed world, which is where only 20 percent of reported cases exist. It is sometimes pointed out that the 94 percent includes the programs of pharmaceutical companies, and that treatments developed will ultimately benefit everyone. But who are they kidding? At a recent international conference, the early morning session was devoted to describing an excellent program of care and accompaniment in the USA. At the coffee break, I found a friend, a Zambian priest, standing in the corridor, quietly weeping. "All that money," he said. "When *we* can't afford *aspirin.*"

The economic policies of the free market, reinforced by those of the World Bank and the International Monetary Fund, have tended to benefit the better-off, but have often further impoverished the poor. The new world economic order, feeding as it does on promoting consumption, depends for its survival on maintaining the categories of consumer and consumed. It's rooted in the hope that those who fall into the "consumed" category won't turn round and bite the hand that fails to feed. Poverty and its products—drug trafficking, crime, civil unrest, HIV—will not stay hidden in the ghetto.

For young people in particular, if life seems to offer nothing in a world where so many have so much, then there's not much to preserve your life *for.* Market and media have created a value system where success has to do with what you own. The short-term attractions of drugs or casual sex are good news if you have nothing else to hope for. And this is just as true in the East End of London, where I live, as it is in the slums of Kampala or the *favelas* of São Paulo.

There is much evidence, within this situation, of the increasing feminization of poverty, of women and girls on the bottom rung of a ladder whose legs are sunk with increasing firmness into the mud, the prime victims within communities which are themselves huddled on the lower rungs. It's naïve to suppose that you can speak of prevention and also be passive or silent before a system that generates poverty.

There is a feeling, though, among those who are not poor (and also, sadly, among many who are) that poverty, though unfortunate, is somehow inevitable, and that the economics of the market are the only option available to us. In Brazil, in Argentina, in India, I heard the fall of the Berlin Wall described as a key event for the whole world. Along with the collapse of communism went a collapse of faith in *any* political agenda other than that dictated by so-called liberal economics. "There is no alternative," the cry goes up. Fear, then, combines with a sense of powerlessness to produce paralysis. Round the slums and shanty towns and refugee camps of the South (and increasingly of the North), new walls rise, built from the dust and rubble of Berlin, 1989. Hidden behind them are the poor, who just might, by their very existence, prove that the dream is not working, the promise a sham, the cost too great.

This situation is not new. The best way to deal with something that's worrying is to make it invisible. In terms of AIDS, there has been a recent effort in the right-wing press to pretend that the pandemic has been grossly exaggerated. There's a striking parallel here in some recent press treatment of threats to the environment. All too frequently, national and international efforts to increase funding for environmental programs, and to promote environmentally desirable practices in industry, are met with derisive comments about prophets of doom, or scare-mongering kill-joys with a hidden political agenda.

Where unwelcome facts are presented to systems (in these cases the structures that control the world's economies) the "powers" that protect those systems come surging into action to protect them. The institutional church, whether it likes it or not, is one of those powers. It tends to be defined, and to define itself, as male, and as "non-poor." Sometimes it has actively benefited from systems that oppress the poor; sometimes, by its silence, it has colluded with them.

Where institutional churches make HIV a priority, or encourage their members to engage in AIDS care and education, it's dishonest for them to do so without reviewing their own positions in relation to poverty. Concern for the virus and those affected by it is not just a pastoral matter. HIV is not like poor housing or bad sewage. It refuses to be confined to a ghetto. Poverty is the catalyst and the compost for a sickness that may threaten us all.

## CHANGE VS CULTURE

In Chapters 4 and 5, we looked at issues of culture generally— in Argentina, the culture of local communities, in Brazil, the role of the media in creating culture and in reinforcing the gender roles men and women adopt.

In Yupa's story, she was forced out of polite society because, in contracting HIV, something had happened for which her culture had no script. It wasn't part of the "story" people believed themselves to be part of. They didn't know how to cope with it, and worse, they didn't know how to handle the questions it raised about their own assumptions. Yupa and her husband were respectable members of the community, pillars of the church. They went on loving each other to the end. They were, in a sense, "without sin." And yet this thing had happened. In terms of the plot, that wasn't how it was supposed to be. Just as respectable society felt threatened by Jesus, Yupa's community felt threatened by Yupa. In Jesus' case on purpose, in Yupa's case inadvertently, both challenged the story-lines of their respective cultures, and therefore had to be written out, as the character played by a sick actor is written out of a TV soap opera.

Maybe it's the nature of culture to create, for its members, a schizophrenic situation in which the cultural "story-lines" take on the status of truth, whatever the evidence to the contrary. They then become so much part of our consciousness that we're not fully aware of their existence. Perhaps truth is always easier to articulate from the margins of a culture, where its central myths have become untenable and people are forced to re-examine them.

And yet God created people as social beings, operating in particular contexts. People are most fully human as embodiments of their own culture, and the incarnate God is present in that full humanity. But it's the nature of all human institutions to create story-lines for themselves, which may or may not reflect the values they say they hold; to build up orthodoxies and authority structures, to develop excluded categories so that we can shout "unclean, unclean," and in doing so, thank whichever god we worship that we are not as others are. It's only by doing this that a culture or structure can do its job, can provide a context that's stable enough for individuals to operate within it. The "powers" that protect it are there to ensure its survival, so cultural and institutional change will always be resisted.

Change, when it does come, may be as a result of war or natural disaster, economic collapse, outside events which the institution has not foreseen, or over which it has no control. When this happens, so many things are thrown into the melting pot that nothing can ever be the same again. But where cultures change from within, it will probably be for one of two reasons. Either the excluded categories (those who don't benefit from the way things are) become so numerous and/or powerful that the authorities can't go on maintaining the status quo; or else a sufficient number of people come to realize that the paradigm beliefs of the culture have become impossible to maintain. Although the former possibility can't be ruled out, it's with the latter that I am particularly concerned in the context of HIV and the insights offered by the experience of women.

Let's say, for the sake of argument, that Yupa's story has challenged two of the paradigm beliefs of any culture: first, that so

long as you keep your hands "clean" in the terms of conforming
to the rules, so long as you obey the eleventh commandment and
don't get found out, then the unthinkable won't happen to you;
and second, that membership of respectable society, which
knows and keeps the rules, is the passport to the best there is in
life. Jesus' story said this wasn't true. But so does Yupa's, because
Yupa has found happiness, and a sense of her own value. Yupa
has found love. She has also found Nong, her second husband
who, like her, is HIV+.

I was once standing in the rain outside Church House in
London, which is the headquarters of the Church of England.
Delegates were gathering for a general synod meeting, and I was
in the front row of a group of nearly a hundred women, quietly
demonstrating on behalf of the Movement for the Ordination of
Women. We who stood at the front carried huge cardboard
letters saying "WAITING." We were bedraggled and frozen.

Then Desmond Tutu walked past with Jim Thompson, who
was my own bishop at the time. They stopped to speak to us.
Tutu, eyes twinkling, looked us up and down. "Smile!" he said.
"It's the first rule. You must always look more cheerful than your
oppressors. It drives them mad!"

It's OK for "the system" to reject you: it's the nature of systems
to create a category of outsiders. Social and political forces create
these categories of undesirables; religious organizations give
moral and spiritual endorsement to their exclusion. Break the
rules, they say, and you're meant to be miserable. What is really
threatening is when those on the outside seem to be having more
fun than the fully paid-up members of the system. So we'll try and
pretend, says the system, that they're not just breaking the
system's rules, but sinning against its god as well. Their happiness
is somehow different from the happiness of the virtuous.

And yet Jesus' claim was that God's future would be *defined* by
the marginalized. These would be the first at the feast, *these* are
the people to whom abundant life is offered. Difficult, isn't it?

Let me introduce you to a friend.

### "Shit to How To!"

Ladeiro da Gloria, in Rio de Janeiro. Up the steep, cobbled
street, through a wrought-iron gate in the rotted greystone wall
and up a flight of narrow steps, there is an old, rambling, ochre-

painted house with window frames of peeling white stucco. It is a shabby building, but warm and welcoming, its doors and windows standing open. On each level there is a terrace: sun-sodden, shaded with apricot trees and palms, oleanders and bougainvillea.

The lower terrace is the hub of the building's life. It looks peaceful, but in fact everyone who enters or leaves the building goes that way. As I do, returning to the meeting after my morning at the beach. In a white chair, in the shade, deep in conversation, is a tall, thin, beautiful man, olive-skinned, with long dark hair, tied back. This is Ernesto Cardoso, director and part-founder of the Brazilian development agency ISER.

Ernesto is a liturgist. He despairs of churches where the liturgy is churned out mechanically, week after week, with no relation to the participants' lives. His mission is to develop ways for people to bring life and liturgy together. His first book, published with Nancy Pereira, is called *New Gestures, New Gazes.* The new one will focus on biblical and liturgical resources around Brazil, relating them to local cooking and food. "Why does liturgy always ignore people's bodies?" he asks. He looks at me piercingly. "Women's bodies in particular. Women are supposed to leave outside the church door all those bits of themselves which couldn't equally well belong a man. Perhaps we should have little pegs to hang them on," he says. "Breast pegs. Womb pegs. And a virus peg for the use of anyone infected with HIV."

Ernesto is a member of the WCC's AIDS consultative committee. He has known for the past six years that he is HIV-positive, and now he has AIDS. Someone has shown him the draft proposal for *Women in the Time of AIDS,* and he likes it. He likes the emphasis on culture, the kairos element. (It was this conversation, most of all, that challenged me to think through the earlier discussion on institutional spirituality.)

All this is useful. But it's not the reason why this seems such an extraordinarily important conversation. In talking to Ernesto, I have the feeling I'm talking to someone with blinding insights to share, someone who lives most immediately in the present, for whom this conversation is the only thing in the world that matters. And yet he is suffering at this moment from pneumocystis, and his cough is never far away.

From the moment when he was diagnosed HIV+ on January 24, 1990, and his despairing cry of "kyrie eleison," he has learned so much. He's learned the reality of pain, for a start, and of physical weakness. He's learned to honor the "divinity of each moment"—the absolute importance of grasping the present and living it to the full. He's accepted the need to allow his body and spirit to set their own pace, resting or writing when the urge is on him. He rejects activism as a way of being. AIDS is a challenge, he says, to *be* more fully, and not to *do*.

The pain and unpleasantness themselves won't let you off this hook, and they mustn't be denied as part of the whole experience. "We need to remember to live," he says, "but at the same time we need to forget to live. Why has pain become such a private thing?" he asks. "Constant diarrhea," he says, "has been the loneliest experience of my life. What help is formal religion with that? Maybe we need a theology of diarrhea," he suggests. His eyes light up, and he gives a shout of laughter. "They'd *hate* that," he says.

He keeps being given books on how to live with terminal illness, how to cope with HIV, how to this and that. "Shit to How To," he says with passion. The opportunity the virus offers is precisely *not* to live according to somebody else's prescription, but to find out what it means to be most fully yourself, present with all your senses at a particular point in time. He thinks Judeo-Christian tradition makes it very easy for Jews and Christians to cave in to How To, because of its emphasis on the omniscient, all-powerful father, present in our subconscious as a long-running, comprehensive How To reference book.

"Why didn't Jesus make a family?" asks Ernesto. "He obviously liked women. Why was he never a father? Because the message of Jesus has nothing to do with How To, it's to do with *being*— being born, being alive, loving, suffering, dying. And to do with accepting and living these experiences, in one's body and spirit, *in time.*"

"Which is where liturgy comes in," I say. His face lights up. "Exactly," he says.

The sun has moved round and our corner of the terrace is becoming uncomfortably warm. Ernesto was intending to go to the airport to collect something, but it is now too late. We return, rather reluctantly, to the subject of our respective books. Would he consider writing an introduction to this one? Both his and mine have to be finished by Christmas. It will be a busy Advent.

Brazil is a football culture, so we promise to operate as supporters, or fans, standing on the sidelines of each other's lives and cheering each other on, Ernesto in the South, me back in England. We practice our football fan-liturgies, with noisy gestures, to the surprise of a couple of serious-looking conference-goers who have dropped out of their meeting for a quick cigarette. Next time I am in Brazil, I promise to visit his home.

We embrace with warmth. And I think to myself, how am I ever, in a million years, going to do justice to this conversation when I come to write it up?

On December 20, 1995 Ernesto died. He never wrote the introduction. Ernesto "Shit to How To" Cardoso, thank you. And rest in peace. Your flame is still alive.

## BODY TALK

Women have appeared in these pages as mothers, wives and girl children, as wage-earners, as copers, as war victims, as refugees, as objects of male fantasy and of sexual and other kinds of violence. They have appeared as commercial sex workers. They have appeared as media creations. They have appeared as the powerless, as the poorest of the poor, as temptresses and virgins.

At the women, AIDS and media conference I attended in Rio, the editor of the Brazilian version of *Marie Claire* magazine said, "You will never stop women getting infected with HIV until you stop them falling in love with men." Everybody laughed. This was the world of women's magazines talking. But she was being serious.

I suspect that for anyone who is deeply in love, at the moment of physical union at any rate, the rules of "safe sex" mean very little. "Being in love" involves surrender; it delights in the body of another, weeps with gratitude for the joy of being found beautiful; it operates in a context of trust.

It also involves control. People fall in love in particular contexts. A dimension of loving somebody is that their welfare, their priorities become yours, too. In Jesus' story, the man who found the buried treasure didn't just buy the treasure, he bought the whole field. In buying into love, one buys into the whole web of existing relationships and commitments that the beloved has. Like dancing or music, therefore, "being in love" is a constant balancing act between control and spontaneity. And there, at the heart of this tension, lies the passion.

In loving like this, there is no part of the beloved to which I want to be closed. It may be compatible with sustained fertility control to the extent that the contraceptive method used does not interfere too much with the spontaneity and mutuality of the surrender. Negotiating safe sex, insisting on the use of condoms, all these oh-so-sensible rules that safe and responsible loving demands—they matter, of course, because causing harm to the beloved is the worst thing I could possibly do, and also because I am an adult, and I know that love has to have a sustainable context if it is to flourish. But the values of this kind of love are values of a different order.

Romantic nonsense? The tale of "true love" is the oldest story in the world. Weepy movies, sentimental magazine stories, the love story that blooms against a backdrop of crime and international intrigue—people lap them up. Are they mere sentimentality? Or does their very popularity reflect a deep longing for it to be true, not just for these fictional characters, but for me? The power of great art, great music, great literature and also, of course, of effective liturgy, is to convince that these "other order" values are in fact the truth; that redemption and love, loyalty and self-sacrifice are the stuff of the real story that is being played out in our universe, although our human preoccupation with getting and spending and surviving generally may distract our attention from it most of the time. In Martha and Mary terms, Jesus says that this story is more important, ultimately, than chopping vegetables. Dream on, Lord, say many women. Do you want your dinner cooked, or don't you? So we slice the carrots anyway, but go on dreaming about love.

The Old Testament is no stranger to the erotic. "As the apple tree among the trees of the wood, so is my beloved among the sons of men. I sat down under his shadow with great delight, and his fruit was sweet to my taste," sings the writer of the Song of Songs. "He brought me to the banqueting hall, and his banner over me was love. His left hand is under my head, and his right hand doth embrace me" (Song of Sol. 2:3-6).

Referring to the "Song of Songs" in his *Letters from Prison,* Bonhoeffer says, "One could hardly have a more passionate and sensual love than is there portrayed." Substantiating this, he refers his reader to Song of Sol. 7:6 (v.7 in newer versions), whereas I respond more to the former. But then he's a man. "It is a good thing," he says, "that this book is included in the Bible, as a protest against those who believe that Christianity stands for the restraint of passion."

Why, then, in the West at any rate, and also in the Christian traditions that were exported to Africa, Asia and Latin America, has mainstream Christianity always been so nervous about erotic love? Attempts to attribute human sexuality to Jesus have been denounced as heresy; the virginity of Mary is reiterated annually, throughout Christendom, in every telling of the Christmas story.

The sin of Adam and Eve is widely believed to be the discovery of their sexuality. But how can that be the case? In the Genesis story, it's not the couple's nakedness that alerts God to their fallen state, it's the realization that they have *discovered* their nakedness. Why the fig leaves? asks God. What is it that has spoiled your relationship with one another? Why have you suddenly become embarrassed before me?

One of God's gifts to human beings is the ability to be happy in their bodies, naked before each other and before God, in absolute confidence that they are lovable and loved. That's the garden-of-Eden state from which we alienate ourselves in listening to the serpent. Eden was finished for human beings as soon as we realized that nakedness was a bad thing. The story of the Fall is the story of the serpent setting woman up as the great corrupter, the destroyer of relationship, the cause of men's alien- ation from God. The shamefulness of the body is somehow connected with the corrupting power of women.

But Eden is, first and foremost, God's celebration of God's own passionate creativity, and God's will that human beings should share it. It wasn't God who kicked us out of Eden. It was in setting up these other rules between ourselves and God that we became aliens there.

It could be argued that the erotic is the most powerful *creative* force in the world. It is, if you like, incarnate love, the body expressing itself creatively in dance, in liturgy, in love for the other. Bonhoeffer explores the idea that the erotic is part of what he calls the "polyphony" of our lives: that the Christian life is one in which the human and the divine, the rational, the affective and the erotic are held together in a kind of controlled and contra- puntal music, whose "ground bass" is God.

The African-American writer Audre Lorde, in her famous essay "Uses of the erotic: the erotic as power" says, "The very word erotic comes from the Greek word *eros*—born of Chaos, and personifying creative power and harmony. When I speak of the erotic, therefore, I speak of it as an assertion of the lifeforce . . ."

Organized religion has tended to see only the Chaos-related aspects of eroticism. Bonhoeffer himself comments on the danger of intense love destroying the polyphony of life. And of course eroticism, like everything else, is corruptible, and may become a means of self-love, of violence, of oppression. Given the predominantly male culture of most organized religion, it would hardly be surprising if wars were to be waged against corrupted eroticism.

What is sad, and also profoundly destructive, is the way that eroticism itself has come to be treated as if it were, by definition, corrupt. In welcoming the erotic, the story goes, you risk the fearful possibility that you also welcome the creative power of women, and the potential for chaos which men may secretly fear in their own sexuality. Best act as if erotic passion were something to be indulged privately, at home. Eve will be kept under control, Adam able to get on with the real business. Observe the shock-horror of many who listened to Chung Hyun Kyung in Canberra. A female God who is erotically creative? How terrifying!

But Chung and other feminist theologians are not concerned, here, with gender analysis, or promoting the ambitions of women as such. They are concerned that in denying the creative power of love, church and world are denying the power and energy of creative passion in bringing about political change. There are some incredibly good and committed people working against poverty, the arms race, abuses of human rights and so forth. Many, today, would acknowledge the need to check programs out for gender bias. All this is to be found in the How To books. But what really motivates these people, inspires them with the energy to go on?

"Of particular importance in our time," says Audre Lorde, "is the reclaiming of the much-neglected, much feared erotic dimensions of love . . . We need to recapture a vision of the divine eros as intrinsic to God's energy, God's own passion for connection, and hence also our own yearning for life-giving communion and our hunger for relationships of justice which makes such fulfillment possible."

This insight could be invaluable to Christian campaigners for social justice, because it helps explain why passion and celebration are better motivating forces than guilt. I have been astonished and very much moved by people's capacity to celebrate in situations of extreme poverty and oppression. Maybe the passion then becomes the effective driving force, and the rules are more easily perceived as relative.

So. Poetry or theory? Energy or the rules? I would say both, or rather all of these. Seventeen years spent teaching literature and creative writing to adults and older children convinced me that human creativity requires disciplines if it's to flourish. But knowing the rules, understanding the disciplines is the driest and most dreary activity in the world if there is no communication of creative energy, no sense that the creator cares passionately for his or her creation.

A creative relationship will be a balance of passion and control. The energy which drives the creativity comes from the passion; but it's given direction and integrity by the control. It seems to have been the nature of organized religion to focus on the need for control while responding in fear and embarrassment to the passion. Sexuality, then, comes to be understood in terms of broken rules—trivial, guilt-provoking, calling into play our most basic and shameful instincts.

This mindset then loses its conscious association with religion and becomes inculturated into the mindset of society. Having taken root there, it provides a license for the abuse of sexuality, the use of power to exploit sexuality for trivial or violent ends. If I don't think my treasure has any ultimate value, if honoring it is just a matter of keeping rules made by other people, if liking it is going to make me feel guilty anyway, then it's not a treasure at all, so why does it matter what I do with it?

There is an urgent long-term need for theology to re-assess the biblical bases of the churches' attitudes to sexuality in general, and in particular, to re-examine the icons of womanhood that 2000 years of Christian theology have left us with. But that's not going to help the generation growing up today in a time of AIDS, often having a much greater understanding of what that means than their parents or teachers or pastors. It's immoral for churches to continue to impose damaging and life-denying atti-tudes to sexuality on these young people. They will either cave in to the dualistic morality they're being fed (the morality of inconsistency and denial described above); or else they'll vote with their feet and take their creative energy somewhere else.

Our Creator formed us, in love, from Chaos, courts us with longing every day of our lives, seeks connection with that God-

given passion and energy within every human being so that we
may be drawn into the great narrative of Creation. It's what we
long for. Where the church draws a delicate veil over the creative
passion and energy that drives its members, it's protecting itself
from God.

## WHOSE STORY?

The idea of a "story" has gained much ground in recent years,
not as fiction but as a tool which helps us analyze and understand
what's going on, and our own place in it. The Great American
Dream motivated a generation in the USA; the Chinese government's single-minded commitment to economic growth provides
a motivating force in whose shadow issues like human rights
become insignificant.

Today, there is a worldwide conviction that the economics of
the free market will solve all our problems. But this, like the
others, is the narrative of the powerful. In the face of these "great
narratives," the stories of the powerless become inaudible, and
structures develop to make sure they stay that way. In defense of
market economics, the poor must be confined to the *favela,* ecol-
ogists are represented as the loony left who want to sabotage
progress and stop people getting rich, refugees and asylum-
seekers are scroungers who must go back home and stop trying
to steal our birthright.

So groups and people who don't benefit from the narrative,
and might therefore disturb our belief in its central claims about
prosperity and choice, are quite simply written out of the story.
The failure of Soviet communism seems to have caused a widespread collapse of the hope that this might ever change. With the
approach of the millennium, economic prophets like Alvin Toff-
ler predict a terrifyingly believable future of more and more rigid
divisions between elite and exploited, consumer and consumed
—a future which has already arrived in some parts of the world.

This narrative depends on the existence of an underclass of
poor people who don't benefit from the system, and who aren't
even mentioned in the sub-plot. The majority of these will be
women. But HIV feeds on situations of hopelessness and poverty. If I'm nobody, who cares what risks I take with my life? If
I'm poor, survival till tomorrow is more urgent than the risk of
long-term infection. If there's no hope of my ever being part

of the culture of consumption which is acted out on the television screen, then I might as well have what pleasure I can while I'm at it.

The narrative assumes that those who write it control what happens, that they are the ones who create the systems of control. But HIV feeds on authoritarian, patriarchal and hierarchical structures. If I have no control over what happens to me, I can't exercise effective moral choice. If someone else makes decisions on my behalf, I lose faith in my ability to make them for myself.

The elite—the ones who are writing the story—make the rules of the game. They are the rules that work for them. And their world is the world of men. But HIV feeds on situations where the rules bear no relation to people's reality. Give me rules and morals which are impossible to keep, and I'm quite likely to give up altogether.

The narrative hits the jackpot when the disempowered can be persuaded to subscribe to an iconography that confuses them, denies them a sense of identity, and appears to justify their oppression. The Eve-Mary spectrum within which women operate in Christian tradition is a case in point. We can never be like Mary, so we must be like Eve. Not surprising, then, that they want to keep us under control. But if I don't know who I am, how can I be expected to take control of my own destiny?

In commenting on Yupa's story, I suggested that there is a "magic circle" from which I risk being excluded if I am caught breaking the rules, a magic circle which is a feature of all the "great narratives" mentioned above. Membership of this circle is the reward I stand to gain by subscribing to the narrative. And I may continue to subscribe, even if I don't benefit from it, because if I obey the rules there is always a chance that I might make it into the circle.

But wasn't Jesus' message one of good news to people *outside* the magic circle? Anna and Barbara in Villa 21 in Buenos Aires were clear about this. It's no use sitting back and waiting for government to do something about it. The new economic order is effectively depriving governments of the ability to govern. Organizing locally, bringing people together, is the way to create a counter-culture whose values are different, to which people bring their will to live abundantly, and their determination to make it happen. "I have made here," says Barbara, "the best friends I have had in the whole of my life."

For reasons set out above, HIV infection puts one outside the magic circle, makes one unacceptable in terms of the dominant narratives of our time and the values they hold. The challenge, then, is to create a new narrative, a story of hope born out of living characters and a real context. Look at Yupa's experience when she joined the HIV project and found people who didn't accept the old values. It became possible to turn her back on the old life. Now she feels loved and cherished. Life has a meaning. She values every minute of every day. Ernesto echoes this; he talks about his escape from the life-denying tyranny of the How To culture into a life where he treasures "the divinity of each moment," the quality of each encounter. Helen and Jim Worth found themselves released into "being in love" in a way they hadn't known before. Florence and the people of Kagoma found new life when they came to realize that the marks of death, and the seeds of new life, are to be found not in the How To books but in their own culture, out of which the energy and creativity for change must come.

Thomas Kuhn, in *The Structure of Scientific Revolutions*, suggests that scientific progress doesn't happen evenly. What happens is that people live within an internally consistent belief system that Kuhn calls a paradigm—the idea that the earth is flat, for instance, or was made in seven days, and the whole set of beliefs that go with these precepts. When evidence starts to emerge that something else might be true, those who are brave enough to say so are regarded as heretics—Galileo, or Darwin, for instance. But gradually, the evidence becomes more convincing, more and more people start to question the old paradigm, until suddenly it seems the mindset of society undergoes a radical shift. *Of course* the world is round. *Of course* it evolved over millions of years. How could we ever have thought otherwise?

One such contemporary paradigm is the "great narrative," mentioned above, of economic progress achieved through the organization of the world according to the principles of the free market. It's a paradigm that's internally consistent so long as I look at it from the point of view of those who benefit, so long as I subscribe to the creed that consumption is the highest value. But post-modern thinking warns me to beware of the power of the "great narratives," to examine the paradigm beliefs of my time in relation to my own context, my own experience of the world, and see if they still make sense.

For Florence in Kagoma, for Ernesto in Rio, for Anna and Barbara in Villa 21, for Yupa in Chiang Mai, the great narrative has exposed itself as a great lie. Therefore they have stopped believing in it. They live by other values. They have ceased to be players in a story that no longer makes sense.

But this, like the road to Jerusalem, is a rough road to tread. Before the resurrection comes the cross. What then about the rest of us, who soldier on inside the magic circle because we can no more get out of it than a camel could go through the eye of a needle?

At the end of the day, it's from inside this dominant narrative that change must come, when the powers that protect it are perceived by those who support them as figments of the imagination, when a paradigm shift takes place in people's understanding of how the world must be, and they are empowered to follow the ingrained knowledge of what is good which exists in all our hearts. Like the Berlin Wall, like the fall of the Marcos regime in the Philippines, like the end of apartheid in South Africa, change comes when the majority of ordinary people reject the narrative's tyranny and refuse to go on colluding with it. Living in faith means living as if we believe that will happen.

So change must come from within. But it's the voices from outside the system that carry the message of life and love and hope which the powers most fear. Hence the ghetto. Hence the shanty town. Living inside the system, welcomed in love by those on its margins whose truths my way of life so often denies, what do those voices say to me?

I listen, and this is what I hear.

First, the basis of true morality isn't a set of rules. It's a commitment to life, that involves learning to love and be true to myself— my real self, and not the self I might become if only I learned to obey the rules. Which in turn involves exercising whatever degree of choice I have to opt into situations and relationships that make it possible to live in love. In this way, I will learn to love God.

Next, it involves choosing life for others. I am not called to change the world. I should not expect to like everyone I meet. But I *am* called to be alert to the powers that diminish and oppress, that cause poverty, that buttress patriarchy, that exploit and manipulate others or destroy the lifeforce that is in them.

Finally, I must have faith. That doesn't mean forcing myself to believe fifteen impossible things before breakfast. It means recognizing that the individual characters in the "great narrative" are ordinary people like myself, so the story can be changed. From the margins come other narratives, built on suffering often, and on poverty and rejection, but good news for all that. They are stories that speak of love, of sacrifice, of resurrection and life. They are stories that speak of purpose and hope. Very often, they are the stories of women.

## CHANGING THE STORY

God, in creating, made order out of chaos, and found it good. God, the book of Genesis suggests, was happy. Creation was a great idea. Maybe, says the virus, our stable-born Jesus-God is the *re-creating* God, acting in human history to reclaim our cultures and institutions by insisting that, if the story doesn't work for the sick and the poor and for those on the margins, then it's not the truth, and must be challenged. The prophetic voice, the one that speaks for this re-creating God, is heard most clearly from the margins. Because that's where the truth is experienced, where the great narratives have lost their credibility, and renewal has become an urgent need.

But re-creation is dangerous. Because the culture, and the powers that protect its central narratives, come surging into action, story-lines blazing, and God incarnate now becomes the Savior God, crucified for intervening to stop that culture self-destructing from within.

In Kagoma and Vellore Town and Villa 21, women and young people and men are organizing to re-create their own cultures, change their own stories. It's a painful process, and involves facing uncomfortable truths. They are doing it because the virus has exposed realities that, if they stay hidden, spell death.

Approached from standpoint of women's health, the challenge of HIV/AIDS is this: to live in love, which is the basis of true morality; to live in life, and not be seduced by the rules; to live in truth, which unlocks the prison of respectability; to live in hope, and not the passive acceptance of a story that our hearts know to be the serpent's lies. And then to act as if we believed that human loving is the highest value, and that relationships of quality are not just our greatest treasure but the place where we meet God.

# BOOK LIST

All the following books, articles and reports have been of use to me in the preparation of *Women in a Time of AIDS*. Some of them are mentioned in the text.

Bang et al., "High prevalence of gynaecological diseases in rural Indian women," *Lancet,* Vol. I, pp. 85-88, 1989.

Becher, Jeanne, ed., *Women, Religion and Sexuality,* Geneva, WCC, 1991.

Berer, Marge and Ray, Sunanda, *Women and HIV/AIDS,* London, Pandora Press, 1993. A huge and useful book, many diagrams and case studies.

Bonhoeffer, Dietrich, *Ethics,* London, SCM, 1978.

*Brazil: A Travel Survival Kit,* Lonely Planet Publications, 1989. A useful series, widely available.

Caipora Women's Guild, *Women in Brazil,* Latin America Bureau, 1 Amwell Street, London E1R 1LU, UK, 1993.

COVIFAC, *SIDA, Mujer y Pobreza,* COVIFAC, Juan Agustin Garcia 2044, 1416 Buenos Aires, Argentina.

Doyal, Lesley, *What Makes Women Sick: Gender and the Political Economy of Health,* London, Macmillan, 1995. An immensely sane, readable book, containing a wealth of references drawn from all over the world. Many of the examples I have used in this book are taken from here.

Gebara, Ivonne and Bingemer, Maria Clara, *Mary: Mother of God, Mother of the Poor,* Maryknoll, NY, Orbis Books, and London, Burns and Oates, 1989.

Gnanadason, Aruna, *No Longer a Secret: The Church and Violence Against Women,* Risk series, Geneva, WCC, 1993.

Gutierrez, Cristina, unpublished thesis on poor women and AIDS in slum areas of Buenos Aires.

Harvey, Nicholas Peter, *The Morals of Jesus,* London, Darton, Longman and Todd, 1991. This excellent and stimulating study is discussed in chapter 7.

111

Kelly, Kevin, *New Directions in Sexual Ethics,* London, Geoffrey Chapman, 1996.

Kierkegaard, Søren, *Fear and Trembling,* London, Penguin 1983.

Lorde, Audre, *Sister Outsider,* Trumansburg, NY, The Crossing Press, 1984.

Mudoola, Dan M., *Religion, Ethnicity and Politics in Uganda,* Kampala, Fountain Publishers.

Panos Institute, *Triple Jeopardy: Women and AIDS,* London, Panos Publications, 1990.

Panos Institute, *The Hidden Cost of AIDS: the Challenge of HIV to Development,* London, Panos Publications, 1992.

Paterson, Gillian, *Whose Ministry?,* Risk series, Geneva, WCC, 1993.

Pereira, Nancy and Cardoso, Ernesto, *New Gestures, New Gazes,* ISER, Ladeira da Glora, Rio de Janeiro, Brazil.

Sobrino, Jon, *Christology at the Crossroads,* Maryknoll, NY, Orbis Books, and London, SCM, 1978.

Tharu, Susie and Lalita, K., *Women Writing in India,* Oxford India Paperbacks, 1995.

Thomas, R.S., *Selected Poems 1946-1968,* Newcastle-on-Tyne, Bloodaxe Books, 1986. The verse quoted in chapter 7 is taken from "Song at the Year's Turning."

Thurston, Anne, *Because of Her Testimony: The World in Female Experience,* Dublin, Gill and Macmillan, 1995.

UNICEF, *State of the World's Children,* UNICEF, 3 UN Plaza, New York, NY 10017, and regional offices. Published annually.

Webster, Alison, *Found Wanting—Women, Christianity and Sexuality,* London, Cassell, 1995.

White, Sarah and Tiongco, Roma, *Doing Theology and Development.* Awaiting publication.

World Bank, World Development Report 1993, Oxford University Press.

World Bank, regular updates on HIV/AIDS activities, World Bank, Washington DC, USA.

World Health Organization, *Bridging the Gaps. Official Report on Poverty,* Geneva, WHO, 1996.

World Health Organization, *AIDS: Images of the Epidemic,* Geneva, WHO, GPA Documentation Centre, 1994. Especially the chapter on Women, Sex and AIDS.